BIBLE VERSIONS

BIBLE VERSIONS

A Consumer's Guide to the Bible

HUGH DUNTON

AUTUMN
HOUSE

DEDICATION
For Britta

ACKNOWLEDGEMENTS

Too long ago I rashly responded to a request made
by Dr David Marshall, editor at Autumn House to
the teachers at Newbold College. I am grateful for
his suggestions and gentle persistence, despite what
seemed endless delays. Dr John Walton of
St Andrews University made perceptive and
constructive criticisms of the draft. The highest
debt of gratitude is owed to my wife, Britta, who has
read and reread, pointing out the cryptic, the
jargon, and even the odd nonsense that crept in
with successive rewriting. Now it's time to tidy up
the garden as a small recompense.

Whatever imperfections remain are solely my
responsibility.

First published in 1998

Copyright ©1997 by Dr Hugh Dunton

British Library Cataloguing in Publication Data.
A catalogue record for this book is available
from the British Library.

ISBN 1-873796-71-4

Published by
Autumn House Limited
Alma Park, Grantham, Lincolnshire
NG31 9SL, England

ABBREVIATIONS

ASV American Standard Version

AV Authorized Version or King James Version, 1611

DNTT Dictionary of New Testament Theology

EBC Expositor's Bible Commentary

EDT Evangelical Dictionary of Theology

GNB Good News Bible, or Today's English Version

IDB Interpreter's Dictionary of the Bible

JB The Jerusalem Bible

LB The Living Bible

KJV King James Version, the AV

LXX Septuagint, the Greek translation of the Old Testament

NAB New American Bible

NASB The New American Standard Bible

NEB The New English Bible

NIDCC New International Dictionary of the Christian Church

NIV New International Version

NJB The New Jerusalem Bible

NKJV The New King James Version

NRSV New Revised Standard Version

NT New Testament

OT Old Testament

RSV Revised Standard Version

TBS Trinitarian Bible Society

TR Received Text or Textus Receptus of the Greek NT

TWOT Theological Wordbook of the Old Testament

W & H Westcott and Hort

Unless stated otherwise texts quoted are from the Authorized Version.

CONTENTS

Which Bible shall I use?

WHY THIS BOOK?

I was prompted to write by the puzzlement, misinformation, and even downright hostility that has greeted efforts to obtain the best possible text in the original languages and then put it into English that is available to the ordinary reader. For it is clearly the intention of the Holy Spirit that the Bible should show us Jesus. It says, 'The large crowd listened to him with delight.' (Mark 12:37, AV, NIV.)

There are around 600 English translations of the Bible or parts of the Bible, about 500 in French. No wonder readers can become confused. 'No man having drunk old wine straightway desireth new: for he saith, The old is better.' (Luke 5:39.) Here is the problem in a nutshell. On the one hand we love the familiarity of the old, yet the language is not one we use in everyday speech, and in some cases may be obscure. Yet Eugene Nida points out that people can learn to accept an archaic language. 'Furthermore, people often take considerable pleasure in religious language they do not understand.'[1] Those who are not familiar with the old may find it difficult, off-putting, musty. There may be too great a gap for some between literary beauty and the world where we live. Some associate archaic language and archaic architecture with an archaic faith. In fact, the Bible centres on the Word, the Living One who is alive for ever and ever (John 1:1; Rev. 1-18).

---

[1]Eugene A. Nida, *Message and Mission. The Communication of the Christian Faith*, Pasadena, CA: William Carey Library, 1960, page 204

CHAPTER ONE

Setting the scene

'Each . . . in his own native language.' (Acts 2:8, RSV.)

William Tyndale (c.1394-1536) believed that 'it was impossible to establish the lay people in any truth, except the Scripture were plainly laid before their eyes in their mother tongue'.[1] Even the ploughboy should understand the Scriptures, he told Cuthbert Tunstall, Bishop of London. Tyndale's detractors feared that the Word of God was too sacred and too difficult to be placed in the hands of the theologically illiterate, and that error might creep into the process of translation from the official Latin text, the Vulgate. The idea of vernacular translations was not new; John Wyclif (c.1329-84) and his followers had worked in English. There were translations into German before Luther, and there were vernacular Bibles or portions in Dutch, Flemish, French, Greek, Hungarian, Italian, Portuguese, Scandinavian (Danish, Norwegian, Islandic, Swedish), Slavic languages (Old Church Slavonic, Czech, Bulgarian, Polish, Russian, Serbo-Croat) and Spanish.[2]

The very existence of the Vulgate, a translation from the original languages into Latin, reaffirmed the principle established by the Old Latin and other vernacular versions that the Bible may be translated and still be the Word of God. 'Its force lies not in the magic of its words, but in the power of its message.'[3] Pentecost set the pattern when the Gospel was given in the many tongues of those visiting Jerusalem. Unfortunately, for centuries the Bible was largely in the obscurity of Latin, which only the educated minority could read. But we should note that the word 'Vulgate' is an indication that Latin was the 'vulgar tongue', the language of the people, even if a second language for many.

Is there a problem with Bible translations?

The number of English translations, and the amount of comment, sometimes very fierce, that these have produced suggest that there is an issue worth examining. The problem presents itself in different forms, according to the theory of inspiration held by the Bible translator/reader. Some believe that any difficulties in the text must have been introduced by copyists, not by the Bible writers. Those who argue for verbal inspiration are not agreed on what this means. Did the Holy Spirit dictate to the writer, were the words divinely given in a process that was not dictation, but exercised control of word, syntax and grammar?[4] Or were the Bible writers 'God's penmen, but not His pen'? Do we really have to assume six denials by Peter in order to reconcile the admittedly differing accounts in the four evangelists?[5]

'Ask for the old paths.' (Jer. 6:16.)

Some fundamentalists will use only the Authorized (AV) or King James Version (KJV), as it is usually called in American usage. There are two possible reasons for this:

First, the supposed correctness of the underlying manuscripts both of the Old and New Testaments. Defence of the so-called Received Text, or Textus Receptus (TR), as opposed to later editions, has been particularly vigorous, partly because the changes have been seen as radical and dangerous.

Second, the faithfulness of the translation. Faithfulness here means adherence to the five fundamentals: the inerrancy of Scripture, the virgin birth of Christ, the substitutionary atonement of Christ, Christ's bodily resurrection, and the historicity of the miracles, or variations on these[6] as outlined in 1910 and later.

Paraphrases, loose or expanded translations of the original, raise both concerns, the original language text and how it has been put into English.

Behind these two basic reasons there often lies a sense of the traditional and familiar ('Give me that old time religion . . . ') having a particular sanctity and authority. Some Catholic traditionalists have had a hard time accepting the new form of the Mass, and the Anglican heart may be with the 1662 *Book of Common Prayer*, even while the head recognizes that the *Alternative Service Book* also has its virtues, especially for a younger generation. The familiar text of the Authorized Version, predominant in English for 300 years, has moulded the language with its phraseology and imagery. The words of the Authorized Version have come to acquire for some an authority of their own. Any other translation is thereby suspect, and religious conservatism says, '"'The old is good.'"' (Luke 5:39, RSV.)

Conspiracy theory, inherent in much fundamentalist and evangelical eschatology, sometimes attributes the most sinister motives to any attempts to revise the traditional Hebrew and Greek texts, or produce a new translation. Such conspiracies may be viewed as driven by historico-critical assumptions, by Roman Catholic manipulation, or more recently, New Age plottings.

Bible translation is no new idea

'But how shall man meditate in that, which they cannot understand?

'How shall they understand that, which is kept in an unknown tongue?'[7]

The Old Testament was translated into Greek in the second century BC, and New Testament writers quoted extensively from this version, called the Septuagint or LXX, though also from the Hebrew text. Sometimes it is hard to see what OT text they used.[8] In the early Church, the LXX, not the Hebrew text, was the accepted version among Gentile Christians especially; they could read Greek, but did not know Hebrew.

Our Lord taught in Aramaic, His native tongue, and ordinary people listened, although that does not mean they always understood Him. Even the disciples could be exasperatingly slow on the uptake (Matt. 15:16; 16:9). Jesus' teaching was not mere surface talk. It required thought. His questions and His parables clung like burrs to the mind, causing reflection and searching. In the absence of written work, Jesus taught to be remembered. The parable is peculiarly Jesus' personal teaching vehicle.[9] His encounters with His opponents show that He understood rabbinic argument (Matt. 22:31, 32; John 10:35). He spoke with authority, and not in the manner of the teachers of His day. Scholars have tried translating the Greek report of Jesus' words back into Aramaic, and the highly memorable style of His teaching is brought out by the use of rhythm and rhyme.[10] It is possible, even likely, that Jesus may also have known Greek, useful in the cosmopolitan community around northern Galilee and into Tyre and Sidon (Matt. 15:21), although there is little evidence that any of the gospel material attributed to Jesus was actually given in Greek.

The evangelists were translators

So even the Master's words come to us in translation. Pentecost set the pattern of the Word of God in many languages when the Gospel was given in the tongues of those visiting Jerusalem. The very existence of a translation from Hebrew into Greek, the rendering of Jesus' Aramaic into Greek, and then translation of both

Testaments into Syriac, Coptic, and Latin, affirmed the principle that the Word of God may be translated and still be the Word of God.

The goal of our journey is an encounter with the God of history, our Saviour, so that with the apostle Thomas, at last casting away his scepticism, we shall say, 'My Lord and my God.' (John 20:28.)

The Bible for the people

Protestant belief in the principle of 'the Bible alone', *sola scriptura*, implies that the Bible is intelligible to the plain reader. The large number of commentaries and guides put out by evangelical and fundamentalist publishers suggests that understanding may sometimes need some assistance. The encouragement to Bible reading given to the faithful by the Roman Catholic Church means that Rome, while not surrendering the teaching authority (*magisterium*), endorses the principle of the open Bible. In practice almost all Protestant communities of faith, while believing in the priesthood of all believers, believe in the authority of the denomination or group to interpret the Bible. The cohesion of a sect, denomination, or Church depends on an agreed core of beliefs, however loosely defined. The nearer to the fundamentalist end of the theological spectrum, the more closely will the denomination or group require adhesion to its understanding by the members. Given the predominant role of Scripture in determining Protestant belief, it is essential that the reader is presented with a text that has the most accurate underlying Hebrew, Aramaic or Greek text translated faithfully into the language of the reader.

An American writer noted that while some translations never become accepted, others endure. The reason seems to be that the language used for the successful versions was 'almost perfectly adapted to express the broad, generic simplicity of the original text. Microscopic accuracy and nicety of expression may be all very well for the student in his closet, but they do not represent the human and divine simplicity of the Scriptures to the mass for whom the Scriptures were written.'[11]

Why do people read the Bible?

There is what we might call reading for feeling. The familiar passages give us a sense of reassurance. We are on well-known territory. As we read, stored emotions and memories surface around the text. We are comforted, or moved, wrapped in a blanket of the known. Paul wrote of the comfort or encouragement of the Scriptures, using a word related to the title 'Comforter' (paraclete) given to the Holy Spirit. (Rom. 15:4.)

Then there is reading with the mind, seeking to be instructed and guided, looking for information on what God has said through Bible writers, 'they were written down for our instruction, upon whom the end of the ages has come'. (1 Cor. 10:11, RSV.)

In this library of sixty-six books, bearing the marks of different human authorship yet all having the stamp of inspiration, there are plenty of puzzles for the intellect. The God who invited us, 'Come now, and let us reason together' (Isa. 1:18), has left many challenges in the complex tapestry of the Bible. These need not shake our faith in God's superintendence in the writing. The Lord who built curiosity into our nature has given us a Bible that challenges us at every level of the mind.

'If . . . my words remain in you . . . ' (John 15:7, NIV.)

Yet all the reading will be of little value unless we meet the Lord. As E. A. Nida remarks, 'The Bible can be the Book of life only when it is translated into life by those who comprehend its transforming message. Its force lies not in the magic of its words but in the power of its message.'[12] 'The word of God is living and active. Sharper than any double-edged sword, it penetrates even to dividing soul and spirit, joints and marrow; it judges the thoughts and attitudes of the heart.' (Heb. 4:12, NIV.) We do not come to pass judgement on the Bible; it judges us, pointing us to the Saviour, and giving us assurance. The ultimate challenge is not to understand everything, but to live according to what we presently understand and to look for further understanding. Augustine and Anselm both wrote of belief seeking understanding. 'I believe in order that I may understand', since the gifts of the Spirit of God are spiritually discerned. (1 Cor. 2:14.)

Call to action or lullaby?

Despite the interest in the newest and latest in gadgetry, in religion there is a strong feeling for continuity. In worship we want to be comfortable with the order of service, so that we can participate intelligently. Many Bible readers cling tenaciously to the version to which they have been accustomed. If we are familiar with a Bible, and have learned passages by heart, why read another translation? Jean-Claude Verrecchia turns the argument of familiarity on its head:

'A Bible one is used to, so that one can recite whole passages, risks no longer being a Bible. What gives the irreplaceable value to this book is its ability to shock, to disturb, and shake-up. Whatever the good version you use, take the risk of letting it surprise you.'[13]

When Jesus spoke of the old wine, He was not arguing that the old is better. In fact, the context shows that He was showing how hard it was for people to accept His new teaching, when they were accustomed to the old.

The old wine was mellow and familiar. The new wine was sharper, disturbing.

The familiar cadences of the AV, as with any centuries-old liturgy, add dignity to worship, yet the sonorous beauty may become valued in itself, so that the meaning is toned down or lost. Form obscures content.

This book is written for those who may be confused about modern translations, perhaps thinking that only the Authorised Version is the true Word. Others may wonder how to choose between a variety of translations. This is a problem not only for English readers, but wherever a long established translation is challenged by a new one.

'It is significant that throughout the history of the Church, the extent of translation and revision has always been directly proportional to the Church's spiritual vitality and dynamic growth.'[14]

---

[1]NIDCC, article, Tyndale; his preface (1530) is printed in Dewer M. Beegle, *God's Word into English*. New York: Harper, 1960, pages 125-127.

[2]IDB 3:771-781.

[3]Nida, page 204.

[4]Kathleen C. Boone, *The Bible Tells Them So: the Discourse of Protestant Fundamentalism*, London, SCM, 1990, pages 23-37.

[5]Harold Lindsell, *The Battle for the Bible*, Grand Rapids, MI: Zondervan, 1976, pages 174-176. This is part of Lindsell's chapter 'Discrepancies in Scripture', pages 161-184.

[6]EDT, page 436.

[7]Preface to the Authorised Version, Olga S. Opfell, *The King James Bible Translators*, Jefferson, NC: McFarland, 1992, page 147; (The whole Preface (original wording) is given in Opfell, pages 143-161, and in Beegle, pages 128-151, with modernized spelling and headings inserted).

[8]The Roman numerals for 70, the traditional number of translators. The date is not known. (IDB 4:273-4).

[9]Joachim Jeremias, *The Parables of Jesus*, rev. ed. London: SCM, 1972, pages 11-12.

[10]T. W. Manson, *The Sayings of Jesus*, London: SCM, 1949, pages 28-35; Craig Blomberg, *Interpreting the Parables*, Leicester: Apollos, 1990, page 96.

[11]Fulton, *Forum*, June 1887, in Benjamin G. Wilkinson, *Our Authorized Bible Vindicated*, Washington DC: privately published, 1930, pages 27, 28.

[12]Nida, page 204.

[13]Jean-Claude Verrecchia, *La Bible, mode d'emploi*, Dammarie-les Lys Cedex: Editions Vie et Sante; Villiers-le Bel, France: Societe biblique francaise, 1995, page 23; my translation.

[14]Nida, page 204.

CHAPTER TWO

The Bible and who wrote it

First encounter

For the first time you see a Bible. It may be bound in black and have the words 'Holy Bible', or 'Bible' on the cover. The very title sets this book apart from other books. 'Sacred Scriptures' is a term you may hear people using, and they may be referring to the Bible, or the sacred writings of other faiths, especially the Koran. So the sacred book of the Christians is the Holy Bible. Why holy and why Bible?

Bible comes from a Greek word originally meaning 'books'. Holy, because the Jewish faith centres round the thirty-nine books of the Old Testament, while Christians accept both the Old and the New Testaments, or covenants. But that only pushes the question one step back. Why should the thirty-nine and the twenty-seven books inside that cover be thought of as holy? Is it just tradition?

When Gerhard Hasel wrote *Understanding the Living Word of God*,[1] the title he chose indicates that the Bible is not a set of texts for mere recitation, but a book to engage the mind. It is not to be closed to all except the scholar. 'I never interpret the Bible, I just recite it,' may be typical of some Bible readers, but is more like the approach to a magical text than the way the Bereans read and searched for themselves (Acts 17:11). 'Living' states that the Word has life. It is the Word of God, not a set of legends, traditions or myths, or even man's speculations about origins, the gods and the inexplicable.

Some may ask, Where is that 'Word of God' found? Is

the Bible the Word of God, or does it contain the Word of God? There is a difference. To choose the latter alternative opens the way for the reader to determine what is and is not the Word of God. For the conservative reader, the whole Bible is God's revelation, not just an encounter where no definite information is given. Conservatives believe that God makes definite statements, or in technical jargon, propositional revelation. 'God spoke to our forefathers through the prophets . . . but in these last days he has spoken to us by his Son.' (Heb. 1:1, 2, NIV.)

Authors known and unknown

Who wrote these books? Some have names, but many do not. Every bookseller and librarian likes to know the author; the Bible doesn't oblige in this respect. How did the books of the Bible come to be written. There are several possible answers.

First, God Himself wrote the whole thing. In fact, the only example that has survived of God's writing is the Ten Commandments on tables of stone (Exod. 20:2:17; 32:16; 34:1), and perhaps the mysterious writing on the wall at Belshazzar's feast (Dan. 5:5, 24-26). Jesus wrote in the dust on one occasion, but no one recorded the words that the wind soon blew away.

Secondly, did God dictate the Bible to various writers? If He did, then did the Holy Spirit use very different styles of language and thought, and varying levels of grammar?

Did the Bible writers have some sort of encounter with God and recorded their impressions of the incident? What then of that clear and frequent assertion: 'The word of the Lord came to me, saying . . . '?

The fourth possibility, and I believe the correct one, is that there was divine-human co-operation. The Bible's own claim is startling:

'All Scripture is God-breathed and is useful for teaching, rebuking, correcting and training in righteousness, so that the man of God may be thoroughly equipped for every good work.' (2 Tim. 3:16, 17, NIV.) 'Above all, you must understand that no prophecy of Scripture came about by the prophet's own interpretation. For prophecy never had its origin in the will of man, but men spoke from God as they were carried along by the Holy Spirit.' (2 Peter 1:20, 21. NIV.)

In another context, Paul wrote, 'We have this treasure in earthen vessels.' (2 Cor. 4:7.)

- God wrote the Bible Himself.
- God dictated it word for word.
- The Bible writers 'met' God and tried to describe the experience.
- The Holy Spirit guided the writers, so that there is divine/human co-operation. The result is still the 'Word of God'.

Even the Lord Jesus accepted the limitations of a human body during the Incarnation. He accepted the limitations of the Aramaic language in teaching heavenly truths. He accepted the limitations of Hebrew and Aramaic in the Old Testament and Greek in the New. In dealing with the human race, God imposes limits on Himself, if one may so express it, since the Divine has to make Himself understood by people, with their limited experience and powers. Imagine the most clever and learned scientist talking to his small children. Everything has to be made as simple as possible. But even then, we, the children, find our minds stretched by what our Father tells us.

What is the Word of God?

To come back to a question raised earlier: Is the Bible the Word of God, or, Is the Word of God found within the Bible? Note the difference. Some would interpret 2 Timothy 3:16 to mean, 'all scripture which is given by inspiration' is profitable, implying that some is not given by God. Is the Word of God objectively there in the Bible, so that it speaks the same fundamental message to all readers? If the Bible is a record of encounters with God, as discussed earlier, then is the reader's experience also an encounter with God through the Bible? A merely subjective encounter that does not make any objective statement, but which has to be understood between the reader and God, mediated through the written Word. Your encounter and mine may be different, for the encounter is subjective. There is no objective truth, some would say.

Ideas of how Scripture interacts with the reader have been affected by modern literary theories.[2] Any theory that places the reader above the writer, and subjects the Word of God to existentialist vagaries, puts the reader at the mercy of Paul's 'every wind of doctrine', and the even wilder storms and waves that Jude describes (Eph. 4:14; Jude 13). If the reader and not the writer decides what a book, article, passage or text means, then we have a virtual free for all, an Alice-in-Wonderland situation. We should not get too excited about literary theories, for they become unfashionable rather quickly.

Inspiration

We need to agree on what we mean by inspiration in the Bible. There are *historical narratives* where the author is not named or known. Luke is the only Bible writer who described his method. It is true that Luke does not mention the guidance of the Holy Spirit, but both in his gospel and in Acts he says so much about prayer and the Spirit, that it goes without saying that he recognized divine-human co-operation (Luke 1:1-4; 'It seemed good to the Holy Spirit and to us.' Acts 15:28, NIV).

Then there is *prophetic inspiration*. 'This is the Word of the Lord', 'the Word of the Lord came to me, saying . . . .' The prophet has no doubt. This is not just an encounter with the Lord, but clear and specific information is passed on. Just how the prophetic voice was heard we are not usually told, although visions and dreams sometimes played a part. However the message came, the prophets were certain of its truth and power, risking life and limb to tell it to others.

There is the inspiration of the poet, as in the Psalms, and of the maker and collector of wisdom sayings (Proverbs). Even a tale of disillusion and a late return to God (Ecclesiastes) has its inspired place.

We have looked at several possibilities:

• A dictated text, inerrant in the autographs, that is, the original manuscripts? Since we do not have the autographs this remains a theory, never provable, never disprovable. We may ask why the God who gave an inerrant text in the first place, allowed discrepancies to creep in.

• The Bible writer recorded his impression of his encounter with God? Then we have no objective standard, and the reader may also read subjectively.

• A purely human production? If so, the Jewish and Christian world has been deluded for thousands of years.

• A divinely-given series of books, mediated through human pens. The consequences of this are:

1. There may be copyists' errors.

2. Events in the gospels, for example, are not given in the order of occurrence, but grouped together as the Holy Spirit led the writer.

3. Accounts of the same event may differ in significant detail. A guiding principle for the reverent reader will be to look for complementarity, not contradiction. In other words the narratives reinforce one another to give a multi-dimensional effect. When accounts are not easily reconciled, the reverent reader does not fret, but rejoices in what is there and recognizes that even the most advanced reader still has much to learn. For the Word Incarnate comes to us as the Word Inscripturate.

4. The Bible is not written in God's words. He is not on trial in the language.

5. The writers reflect differing levels of spiritual maturity.

6. We cannot talk of differing levels of inspiration, though we may recognize differing types of religious experience in the writers.

7. The Bible was given for practical purposes.

8. It is the inspired Word of God, the only rule of faith and practice.

9. No one will go astray if following its teachings.

10. It is just as God wanted it to be.

Crank and critic

At the non-Christian or quasi-Christian end of the spectrum are writers who claim to have access to sources which undermine traditional Christian understanding, and produce pseudo-scholarship, for example about the Holy Grail, or claiming a French tomb for Jesus.

Other writers claim that new discoveries of 'Gnostic' gospels, notably the Nag Hammadi finds of 1945-46, show that the NT account of Christianity is incorrect. The conspiracy theory is invoked to argue that the Church suppressed its Gnostic rivals, who may have been the true heirs of Jesus. Theories come, make a splash, and then peter out. Who today remembers or regards John

Allegro's thesis that Jesus and His followers were in a hallucinatory mushroom cult?

Even from academic theologians there is too much barren study of the Bible.

'From within the biblical traditions we must insist and confidently expect that the more profoundly and validly we understand and interpret the Bible, the greater the religious depth with which it will challenge and speak to us . . . . We are confronted with the paradox of a way of studying the Word of God out of which no word of God ever seems to come.'[3]

E. L. Mascall writes bitingly of critical clerical academics who argue for the mythical nature of the Gospels, destroying the reader's faith, offering instead 'existential challenges through which one might achieve authentic self-understanding'.[4] You may very well complain that you do not understand what 'existential challenges' and 'authentic self-consciousness' mean, and there seems to be no cross, no Saviour, no resurrection. But such stones are offered for bread.

Twenty years later seekers old and young might be offered insights into discovering the cosmic consciousness and be urged to look inside themselves to discover whatever they need to find, somewhere within the many aspect of the New Age movement.

A. N. Sherwin-Williams, a distinguished Roman historian, was surprised that historians give far greater credence to their documents, than many Bible scholars do to the authenticity of the Scriptural record.[5]

'Men moved by the Holy Spirit spoke from God.' (2 Peter 1:21, RSV.)

Criticism is mistaken when it treats the Bible as a merely human production. It can be valuable when source criticism and redaction (the editorial process in

Bible writings) criticism are reverently applied. That is, when the superintendence of the Holy Spirit and the integrity of the documents is recognized. When false and unnecessary criteria are created for biblical studies, then scholars are on circular reasoning paths of their own creation.[6] The reader is judged by Scripture. It stands over the reader. For example, will a study of how Matthew, Mark and Luke have dealt differently with the same stories bring out an insight that will give us something to pray about, something to share with others? It can, and should, but only if we go as seekers and learners. It is of little value to go down deep if we come up dry.

These preliminaries may help earnest Christians who are troubled by discrepancies, for example, in numbers between Kings and Chronicles, or by the differing wording given for the inscription over the cross.

> 'If our love were but more simple
> We should take Him at His word
> And our lives would be all sunshine
> In the sweetness of our Lord.'
> — *Frederick W. Faber*

---

[1]Mountain View, CA: Pacific Press Publishing Association, 1980.
[2]Tremper Longman III, *Literary Approaches to Biblical Interpretation*, Leicester: IVP, 1987, pages 13-17.
[3]J. V. Langmead Casserley, (no fundamentalist), quoted in Leon Morris, *Studies in the Fourth Gospel*, Exeter: Paternoster Press, 1969, page 10.
[4]E. L. Mascall, *Theology and the Gospel of Christ*, London: SPCK, 1977, page 102
[5]Mascall, page 70.
[6]Mascall, page 88 ff.

CHAPTER THREE

The contemporary message

'"Write . . . to be easily read."' (Hab. 2:2, JB.)

'So they read in the book in the law of God distinctly, and gave the sense and caused them (the people) to understand the reading' (Neh. 8:8) or 'Ezra read from the Law of God, translating and giving the sense, so that the people understood what was read' (JB). Ezra made sure that the people would hear and understand. The message was given in the language of the people. 'I endeavoured to make Moses sound so German that no one would ever suspect he was a Jew' (Martin Luther on his Bible translation).

The English language has developed over the centuries. Anglo-Saxon, the language of the tribes who invaded Britain as the Roman Empire collapsed, was enriched by the Vikings with Norse words such as 'law', and the place names ending in 'by' and 'thorpe'.

Enter William, exit Harold

The year 1066 and all that brought in Norman French as the language of the ruling classes and government. Old English remained as the speech of the less privileged. The well-off ate pork and beef (Norman-French words) while the peasant knew them only as the swine and bulls and cows he had to look after. Gradually the languages blended to form Middle English, the language of Geoffrey Chaucer (c.1340-1400) and John Wyclif (c.1329-84). By 1611, the date of the Authorized Version aka the King James Version of the Bible, we are into the Modern English period. However, language is not static. Words are born, flourish and fall into disuse. The Anglo Saxon translations by King Alfred the Great are unintelligible to all but specialists.

'God lufade middan-eard swa thaet he sealde his ancennedan sunu, thaet nan ne forweorthe the on hine gelyfth ne haebbe thaet ece lif.' (John 3:16, Anglo-Saxon, simplified by replacing obsolete letters.)

'Forsothe God so louede the world that he gaf his oon bigetun sone, that ech man that bileueth in to him perische not, but have euere lasting lyf.' (Wyclif, 1382.)[1]

'God soo loved the worlde that he gave his only sonne for the entent that none that beleve in hym shuld perisshe: Butt shulde hav everlastyng lyfe.' (Tyndale, 1526.)

The ever-changing language

Wyclif's Bible could have been read by people of Tyndale's time, and if the spelling is modernized, Tyndale is easily read by those familiar with the AV. The story of language is one of both continuity and change.

There have been further changes in the nearly four centuries from 1611 to our own time. The AV was modelled on earlier translations, and was dated even in 1611. The sonorous yet vivid language, very faithful to the text as of the original languages as they had them, has shaped the English language, both in word, idiom and proverb. However, there are hundreds of obscure words and usages in the AV which present a considerable hurdle for the modern reader. Not all traditionalists would find it easy to explain the meaning of obsolete words and phrases. The very beauty and familiarity of the AV text may blind us to the fact that we do not understand all that is being said. Try Mark 6:21; 2 Corinthians 6:12; 8:1; Acts 21:15 for meaning.

Four principal causes of difficulty

1. *Same word, different meaning.* Some words which are still in use today have changed their meaning. For example, 'leasing' (Ps. 4:2) meant lying, not an agreement about property; 'prevent those which are aleep' (1 Thess. 4:15) meant to go ahead of, to precede, not stopping them from doing something; 'talents' denoted a coin in the AV. The AV 'publican' did not run a pub, but collected taxes. 'Reins' (Ps. 7:9) has nothing to do with horses.

'Bowels' was for Paul the seat of compassion, but can sound like a clinical condition (2 Cor. 6:12; Col. 3:12). More startling is the case of the Shunamite maiden. 'My beloved put in his hand by the hole of the door, and my bowels were moved for him.' (Song of Sol. 5:4.) Jeremiah spoke of his liver when we would today speak of the heart as the seat of the emotions (Lam. 2:11).

A 'bushel' (Matt. 5:15) might be remembered today as an out-of-date measure, but not something that could be put over a lamp. 'By and by' could have the meaning immediately. Its present sense suggests the human tendency to put things off. 'Anon' (Matt. 13:20) has gone the same way, so far as it survives today. The 'feebleminded' (1 Thess. 5:14) were not intellectually challenged, but just timid. Other examples are 'took up our carriages' — literally 'having made ready' (Acts 21:15); 'roaring' (Ps. 22:1), better translated as groaning; 'chief estates' (Mark 6:21), meaning leaders. Purge means prune (John 15:2), or purify in other contexts. 'Conversation' equals 'way of life'; 'mansions' (John 14:2) means 'rooms' (RSV, NIV), a 'place of halt on a journey'.[2] It does not mean mansion in the modern sense, despite the ideas of heavenly riches it has conjured up to the AV reader.

I once heard a zealous and supposedly educated preacher declare that Joshua and his troops were not ignorant men, they had scientific instruments, and to prove his point he quoted part of Joshua 15:3, 'fetched a compass'. Had he read the verse carefully he would have seen that it was the boundary line that went round, not Israelites checking directions. It might have been slightly more plausible if he had argued from Acts 28:13, where Luke says, 'we fetched a compass', but the context makes the meaning clear.

Jonathan's artillery was his bow and arrows, not some early cannon (1 Sam. 20:40). Paul's ode to Christian love (1 Cor. 13) in the AV has 'charity', echoing the Latin *caritas*. But the warmth seems to have drained out of the word, so that 'cold as charity' has become a proverb, redolent of grim Dickensian do-gooders.

2. *Forgotten words.* The second group consists of words that have dropped out of today's English. This would include old weights and measures, both English and ancient. The second person singular has died out in all but dialect and church usage, and is difficult with its 'saiths', 'doths' and 'doeths'. 'Trow' (Luke 17:9) is an example of an obsolete word.[3]

3. *Technical terms.* The third group consists of words not widely understood in a theologically uneducated age, such as righteousness, justification, propitiation, expiation, sanctification. These are valuable expressions of deep concepts, but ideas may appear beyond understanding when wrapped in long words with many syllables. Words are like currency in that we have to know the value before making an intelligent decision. How many of us have stood with a handful of unfamiliar notes and coins, trying to work out if the item in a shop is cheap or dear in sterling terms. Language continues to evolve. We date ourselves by our colloquialisms. That is why new editions of standard dictionaries appear. This is not just a problem with English. The French spoken fifty years ago is not the

French spoken today.[4] The same applies to German and the Scandinavian languages, among others. While some are attracted to an older style, others find it musty, and feel that if religion must be expressed in obsolete language then it can have little to say to the contemporary world.

Talk at my level

Translators should take into consideration the vocabulary of the target readership. There is not just one reading public. The wide spectrum of newspapers indicates that. Then there are millions for whom English is a second language. The Bible must be made as clear as possible in the context of the reader. Both Matthew and Luke tell the story of the two house builders, but only Luke mentions digging deep and laying a foundation. This made the story clearer to his readers in parts where foundations were customary. In Palestine the rock was usually already near the surface (Matt. 7:24-27; Luke 6:48, 49). In the story of the paralyzed man lowered through the roof, only Luke mentions tiles, more usual in the areas for which Luke wrote than the common Palestinian roof of poles and dried mud (Mark 2:4; Luke 5:19).

Aramaic words spoken by Jesus or His followers are sometimes quoted, but always with a translation. The writers, guided by the Holy Spirit, wanted the Bible to be accessible and understandable to ordinary people, not locked away in unfamiliar words and style. Yet because the Bible is the Word of God, the dignity of the original should not be sacrificed by misguided attempts to reduce it to the lowest common denominator of understanding.

Even modern translations may lapse into uncommon words, for example, 'bedizened' (Rev. 17:4, NEB) when a more user-friendly word could have served without loss of clarity.[5]

4. *Not enough full stops.* The fourth difficulty lies with the sentence structure of the originals. The AV translators were used to long sentences in English, so were not put off by such examples in Greek as:

'And supper being ended, the devil having now put into the heart of Judas Iscariot, Simon's son, to betray him; Jesus knowing that the Father had given all things into his hands, and that he was come from God, and went to God; he riseth from supper, and laid aside his garments; and took a towel, and girded himself.' (John 13:2-4.)

This is far from how a modern writer would create a sense of quiet but intense drama. Modern translations break up the one long sentence.

When Jesus spoke the large crowd listened, and the learned who tried to trap Him in His words 'were amazed', and 'astonished' and silenced by His answers (Matt. 22:22; Luke 20:40). Nicodemus, *the* teacher in Israel, (John 3:10) ultimately became a disciple. Jesus drew all sorts and conditions of people in language suited to their level of understanding. Compare the profound discourses recorded by John with the deceptively simple and memorable parables of Matthew, Mark and Luke. All this was contemporary. Today it needs to be both a contemporary message, yet one that brings to life events of 2,000 years ago.

---

[1]Wyclif, 1382; James Bosworth, *The Gospels: Gothic, Anglo-Saxon, Wyclif and Tyndale Versions*, London, 1907, pages 452-3.

[2]DNTT, 3:229-3 'an abode' 'mansions' in W. E. Vine, *Expository Dictionary of New Testament Words*, London: Oliphants, 1975.

[3]Further examples in Beegle, pages 55-61; IDB 3:583-588 lists over 700 changed and obsolete words.

[4]Verrecchia, page 12

[5]See also, Pearl Sjoelander & Jan Rye, 'How clear is a simplified version?' *Bible Translator*, 33/2 (April 1982), 223-229. G. A. Riplinger has listed words where modern translations use more difficult words than the AV, *New Age Bible Versions*, Chino, CA: Chick Publications, 1993.

CHAPTER FOUR

Over the language barrier

'*The most fascinating thing about translating is that it is so impossible.*' Professor T. H. Robinson[1]

'Caesar did not write nonsense'

Many a young student faced with a piece of translation either into or from a foreign language, would agree with the Professor on the impossible aspect, but not be so certain about the fascination. My patient Latin teacher assured me that whatever garbled (or garbage) version I produced, the fault was not with Caesar or Virgil.

A translator has to make a series of decisions as he faces the original language and seeks to make the content intelligible for readers in another language, and perhaps another culture. The grammar and sentence structure of the biblical languages are different from modern English, so a word-for-word translation would often be quite unnatural or even meaningless. At any rate, it would not be English. Some idioms sound ridiculous when literally translated. 'Eating dandelions by the roots' is the French equivalent of 'kicking up the daisies'. Try 'to put someone in a box', 'that's not my onions', 'he's got a spider on the ceiling'. These are all French idioms, according to the book in front of me designed to help the French find English equivalents. That's the point; equivalent idioms must be found. Just to translate the words makes strange reading.

Order word, or word order?

The word order of Hebrew, Greek and English is very different. 'For not sent the God the Son into the world that he might judge the world, but that might be saved the world through him.' (John 3:17.) This is faithful to the word order of the Greek, but it is not English usage. Not only is the word order different, but thought patterns vary from language to language, especially when they are widely separated by time and space. Yet the translator who believes that the Bible was given by 'inspiration of God', and that 'holy men of God spoke as they were moved by the Holy Spirit' (2 Tim. 3:16; 2 Peter 1:21), has to decide how to bring across the meaning of the original language to the receptor language, for example, Hebrew to English. While the language barrier keeps us from hearing the *ipsissima verba* (the words themselves, the original words), translation should enable us to hear the *ipsissima vox* (the true voice, the voice itself).

Why should there be new translations?
First, the Bible is a text of unique value and should be as accessible as possible, even as language changes over the years. The discovery of new manuscripts, both sacred and secular, sheds new light on the text and background of the Scriptures. The progress of the philological sciences (study of language and languages), and the development of theories of translation give new insights into how to communicate across language barriers.

There are differences in interpretation. It is not always easy to decide between different senses of a word or phrase in the original to discover the author's meaning. Lastly, theological concerns may influence translation.[2]

Alternative translations
A text may be translated several ways according to the grammatical form and textual variant adopted by the translator. Where there are possible ambiguities in the

original text, the AV gives marginal or footnote alternatives.

Habakkuk 2:4 is quoted in Hebrews 10:38 (LXX), where the meaning of the Hebrew *emunah* is 'faithfulness'. Romans 1:17 and Galatians 3:11 emphasize righteousness by faith, rather than living faithfully.[3]

Confessional and cultural factors are the origin of some translations. For example, Luke 23:43 may be punctuated to read 'I tell you the truth, today you will be with me in paradise', or 'I tell you the truth today, you will be with me in paradise'. Both translations are equally valid according to the underlying Greek. Theological conviction will determine the translation adopted. Another example of an ambiguous text is Matthew 27:54. Did the centurion confess belief in '*the* Son of God', or 'a son of God'? The Greek has no article. 'The son of God' may suppose more theological understanding than the soldier possessed at that time. Did anyone, even the disciples, understand the deity, the unique Sonship of Jesus, before the resurrection?

The NIV begins Colossians 3:1 with 'since' in preference to the AV 'If', both from the same Greek word. Many will prefer the thought of 'since', as the apostle shows the consequences of being risen with Christ, rather than raising a doubt. The Greek of John 5:39 can be read both as a command and as a statement of fact. The translator must decide on the meaning in context. Should the translator decide on a particular meaning where the original is ambiguous, presumably deliberately so?[4]

Four questions for a translator

A would-be Bible translator has to decide four basic questions:

1. The **type of translation:** Literal or Formal, Dynamic Equivalence, Paraphrase.

2. The **main purpose of the translation:** private devotional reading, a study Bible, a version for liturgical use, a simplified version, or a literal transcription stuffed with archaisms.

3. The **style to be used** in the receptor language, in this case, English. This will be decided to a great extent by the answers given to point two above. Should the style be fairly uniform throughout, as in the AV? Should the style reflect the style and mood of the writers, as far as consistent with English usage? Should a distinction be made between singular and plural (Thou, You), especially when addressing the Deity? How far can the English be up to date, yet not likely to become very rapidly out of date if passing colloquialisms are used? How far should sentence structure and vocabulary be tailored to particular readerships? The AV has a high percentage of Anglo-Saxon-based words, avoiding the excessive enthusiasm for Latinate forms common among some writers of the period.

The original style

Bible writing often shows the background of the writers. Style varies from the lofty to the earthy, from prose to poetry. The AV on the whole uses dignified language throughout. Yet a closer look will show the differences between the books of down-to-earth Amos and the courtly Isaiah. Mark writes in a rugged Greek which reflects the sense of urgency that runs through his gospel. Should the translator faithfully keep every use by Mark of 'immediately' (*euthus*), or remove a few for stylistic reasons? The once fashionable criticism of Mark's Greek has given way to a realization that his Greek serves his purposes. The link word 'and' is much more common in Hebrew constructions than in English.

Should the translator retain it in every instance, or only when natural-sounding English requires it?[5]

> 'It was in the third hour,
> and they crucified him.'
> (Mark 15:25.)

brings out the starkness of that awful scene far more than the bland, 'It was the third hour when they crucified him.' (NIV.) In Mark one can almost hear the hammer blow at the end of each short line.

Idioms

How far should expressions and figures of speech which sound strange in English be changed to an English idiom? What is the translator to do with customs that may not seem suitable in another culture? Paul's advice to greet with a holy kiss seemed more acceptable to the Anglo-Saxons of 1947 when expressed as, 'A handshake all round, please!' (2 Cor. 13:12, J. B. Phillips.)

Some biblical idioms do not translate. Has there been some academic scandal if the deacons have used their office to 'purchase to themselves a good degree'? (1 Tim. 3:13.) Clearly, the translator has to find another expression. 'Strike hands' 'referred to the ancient custom in which a person interceded in behalf of another by providing bail until a trial could be arranged'.[6] The reader might work out some idea of the meaning from the previous 'put me in a surety with thee', though that in itself is not the clearest. Modern versions sometimes use 'recline' at a meal, rather than sit. Since Westerners sit at table, how should the thought be translated? 'Sat' is not accurate; 'reclined' might suggest slouching to readers who were brought up to sit up straight, elbows off the table (Luke 7:36, 37).[7] Sometimes the Hebrew/Aramaic idiom slows us down and forces us to think about the occasion. Compare, 'And he opened his mouth and taught

them, saying . . . ' with 'he began to teach them, saying
. . . ' 'he began to address them. And this is the teaching
he gave:' and 'Then he began to speak. This is what he
taught them:' (Matt. 5:2, AV, NIV, NEB, JB.) The formula
translated literally in the AV appears elsewhere, and is
used in solemn contexts when truth is to be revealed
(Matt. 13:5; Acts 8:35; 10:34; cf Job 3:1; 33:2). The use
of the formula alerts the reader to the seriousness of the
occasion. The NIV does not do this. There is more of the
sense of an event in the NEB and JB.

'With desire I have desired' is a Semitic expression used
for emphasis. 'I have eagerly desired'; 'I have longed.'
(Luke 22:15, AV, NIV, JB.)

Imagine the problems of translating into a language
where words for snow, wool or camel do not exist, to say
nothing of abstract concepts such as justification, repentance and salvation.

Poetry

In translating Hebrew poetry, characterized by
parallelisms, Ronald Knox believed, 'What the reader
wants, I insist, is to get the illusion that he is reading, not
a translation, but an original work written in his own
language, and to our notions of poetic composition, these
remorseless repetitions are wholly foreign. When you
have read a page or two they begin to cloy'.[8] Not everyone would agree. Knox was used to an educated literary
tradition. In oral cultures repetition is important. Familiar
and repeated phrases are part of the bardic tradition and
of stories for young children.

4. **What original language text** should be the basis of
the translation? Texts will be discussed in Chapters 5 and
6. As a preview, we may mention five basic types of NT
text used:

- The Vulgate, in its revised form, as commissioned by

Pope Pius IX, is still the official Roman Catholic text for use in the Vatican's official Latin documents.
- The Textus Receptus, which underlies Tyndale and his successors, including the AV.
- The Westcott and Hort text, the basis of the Revised Version.
- Later texts such as the successive editions put out by the United Bible Societies and Nestle-Aland which incorporate discoveries made after Westcott and Hort.
- Eclectic texts, where the translators have not tied themselves to any critical edition, but selected what they considered to be the best readings from a variety of sources.

Three basic types of translation
1. **Formal or literal,** where as far as possible the original is translated word for word. The Authorised Version (1611), and modernizations of the AV, such as the New King James Version (1982), Revised Version (1881), American Standard Version (1901), Revised Standard Version (1952) and New Revised Standard Version (1989), and New International Version (1978) are all in varying degrees formal translations. The New American Standard Bible (1971) is prepared to allow some ambiguity for the sake of staying faithful to the original.

Literalness can be carried too far. The first Wyclif translation followed the Latin constructions and word order of the Vulgate, and so sounded very unnatural in English. John Purvey made the second Wyclif translation on the principle that 'the best translating is out of Latyn, into English, to translate after the sentence (ie., meaning), and not oneli after the wordes, so that the sentence be as opin, either openere in English as in Latyn'.[9] Duthie cites some modern examples where literalism has been followed at the expense of English style and readability.

Are 'whited sepulchres' readily understood without some background knowledge?[10]

Strict literalists might note that some English expressions have come into the AV that are not found in the Greek: 'God forbid', 'cast the same in his teeth' (Rom. 3:4; Matt. 27:44). This point is seldom raised by defenders of the AV. In an attempt to be faithful to the originals the AV uses italics to indicate words supplied to make coherent English. The practice began with Sebastian Munster in 1534 in his Latin Old Testament. Not even the two editions of 1611 were consistent, and the revisions of 1629 and 1638 did not improve things. Pronouns — he, him, she, her — can cause problems. 'And he spake unto his sons, saying, Saddle me the ass. And they saddled him.' (1 Kings 13:27.) Who got saddled if you follow the grammar, not the sense?[11]

There is much to commend formal equivalence, provided it does not go to the extreme length of arguing that every Hebrew, Aramaic, or Greek word must be translated, and no other words used, regardless of the English style. It is surely too much to argue from 2 Timothy 3:16 that 'all those words were individually God-breathed'.[12] Gerrit Verkuyl, the force behind *The Modern Language Bible*, sought 'as far as possible . . . a complete translation of every word in the Bible'. This resulted in some 'unidiomatic . . . and, at times, wooden language', but this was smoothed out in the 1969 revision.[13]

Beegle writes, 'One word corresponds to many, indicating the limitations of word for word translations. The Revised Version (1881 and 1885) and the American Standard Version (1901) aimed to reproduce as far as possible the word order, idioms, and feelings of the Greek and Hebrew.' The result is something of an 'interlinear translation . . . valuable for those who (not knowing Hebrew or Greek) wish to do detailed, careful study of the Bible in English'.[14] He goes on to give the example of Genesis 12:14, where the Masoretic text, word for word, is almost incomprehensible in English. His NT example is Luke 12:20, 'Said but to him the God, Fool, this night the soul of you they require from you.'[15]

In discussing the word *nephesh* (soul), Fudge notes that 'English translators have rendered it 95 different ways'.[16] Of course, most words do not have 'such a rainbow of shades'. The example of *nephesh* shows how easy it is for the translators to feed back their personal beliefs into the original. The width of meaning and varying contexts of the word made it necessary to interpret. On the whole the men of 1611 used a minimum of interpretation.

2. **Dynamic Equivalence** seeks to convey the meaning of the original without the restrictions of a more formal translation. Examples of this type are the New English Bible, and the Good News Bible, otherwise called Today's English Version. Eugene Nida of the American Bible Society stated; 'To translate is to try to stimulate in the new reader in the new language the same reaction to the text the original author wished to stimulate in his first and immediate audience.'[17] Hilaire Belloc said the question was not 'How shall I make this foreigner speak English?', but 'What would an Englishmen have said to express the same?'[18]

A minor example would be where the original weights, measures, money and the reckoning of time are given in modern equivalents. The six stone water jars at the wedding in Cana held 'twenty to thirty gallons', rather than the 'firkins' of the AV (John 2:6, RSV, NIV, JB). Acts 20:7 (NEB) is translated as 'Saturday night', which appears to be the meaning, but is not in the Greek, which reads, 'on the first day of the week'. The Jewish day begins at sunset.

There are three aspects of equivalence: stylistic, the

referential meaning of symbols, and the conceptual meaning of the symbols.[19]

As an example of stylistic equivalence Nida quotes the Scottish metrical psalms, where the style of the translation follows as closely as feasible the style of the original. The Hebrew psalms were written to be sung, so was the Scottish psalter. The Scottish version uses rhyme as that is part of the Western poetic tradition.

> 'The man hath perfect blessedness
> who walketh not astray
> In counsel of ungodly men
> nor stands in sinners' way.'[20]

The referential meaning of symbols concerns what these symbols refer to in Old or New Testament times. J. B. Phillips gave priority to the conceptual feature of symbolism, trying to bring out the meaning of the text in the clearest way. This may mean substituting or changing the idiom.

Sometimes the original language can be translated in more than one way. For example, in John 1:9, does 'coming into the world' belong to 'man' or 'light'? 'The light coming into the world lights every man' or 'the light lights every man who comes into the world'?

Should Romans 8:28 read 'all things work together for good to them that love God' (AV), or 'in everything God works for good with those who love him' (RSV)? Both readings are possible from the original, but many might feel that the second reading is more positive, as it emphasizes the role of God rather than events. Bible translators recognize that there is a core of verses where alternatives seem equally admissible.

The Trinitarian Bible Society translators consider dynamic equivalence 'a noble goal; however, it is attempted with little regard to the wording of the Hebrew texts. The actual words are no longer considered to be as important as the thoughts behind them . . . . How can the thoughts of a first-century writer be known or conveyed if not through his words?'[21] Dynamic equivalence translators would argue that the TBS have missed the point.

3. **Paraphrase** does not attempt literalness, or close dynamic equivalence. The paraphrase may seek simply to make plain the meaning of the text in modern speech, building clarification of ideas into the text, rather than using marginal or footnotes. It is by its very nature more likely to be interpretive than the previous two types. The difficulty for the paraphrase reader is not knowing when scripture leaves off and interpretation takes over. Gerrit Verkuyl wrote that paraphrase 'leads so readily to the infusion of human thought with divine revelation, to the confusion of the reader'.[22]

4. There is a possible **fourth category**, the method adopted by Alfred Kuen for the French *Parole Vivante*, subtitled 'a synthesis of the best current versions'. Kuen's work is neither direct translation from the Greek, nor paraphrase. 'Instead we have sought to encompass within this translation all ways of understanding the original, yet it contains only thoughts and expressions already found in one or more serious translations. All variations were closely examined in the light of textual criticism of sources and, if they came from too free a version, were put aside or placed in the notes.'[23]

The boundaries between the various types of translation are not rigid. Every translation is to a greater or lesser extent interpretive.

---

[1]cited in Nida, page 189.
[2]*Parole Vivante*. La Bible transcrite pour notre temps par Alfred Kuen, Editeurs de Litterature Biblique, Chaussee de Tubize 479, B.1420 Braine-l'Alleud, Belgium, pages 8-10.

[3]Beegle, pages 100-102.

[4]Jean C. Margot, 'Should a translation of the Bible be ambiguous?' *Bible Translator*, 32/4 (Oct. 1981) 406-413.

[5]'Authentic style and the Truth' , Beegle, pages 73-89; Calvin D. Linton, 'The importance of literary style', in Kenneth L. Barker, *The Making of a Contemporary Translation, The New International Version*, London: Hodder & Stoughton, 1987, pages 19-43.

[6]Beegle, page 109.

[7]Beegle, pages 110, 111.

[8]Beegle, quoted in Sakae Kubo and Walter Specht, *So Many Versions. 20th Century English Versions of the Bible*, Revised edition, Grand Rapids, MI: Zondervan, 1983, page 64; Barclay M. Newman, 'Biblical Poetry and English Style', *Bible Translator*, 44/4 (October 1993), 405-410.

[9]cited in Kubo, page 342.

[10]Alan S. Duthie, *How To Choose Your Bible Wisely*, Swindon: Bible Society, 1995, pages 128, 129.

[11]Beegle, page 112.

[12]Duthie, pages 57, 58.

[13]Kubo, page 82.

[14]Beegle, page 106.

[15]Beegle, pages 108, 109.

[16]Edward W. Fudge, *The Fire that Consumes*, Carlisle: Paternoster, 1994, page 25.

[17]in Kubo, page 174.

[18]quoted in Ronald Knox, *On Englishing the Bible*, London: Burns Oates, 1949, page 19.

[19]Nida, page 189.

[20]Psalm 1, in Nida, page 192.

[21]*The Trinitarian Bible Society, An Introduction*, London: Trinitarian Bible Society, 1992, np.

[22]Kubo, page 92.

[23]*Parole Vivante*, page 12.

CHAPTER FIVE

The Manuscripts and the Canon

The Old Testament: Masoretic Hebrew text and the Septuagint Greek text

The Hebrew Old Testament text mainly used until this century was preserved through the work of Jewish scholars, the Masoretes, from AD 700. There are few manuscripts that could be dated earlier than the ninth century, before the discovery of the Dead Sea scrolls, or Qumran Manuscripts (1947). Work on the Qumran documents has been slow, because of the fragile nature of the materials. However, what has been published to date shows the soundness of the Old Testament Masoretic text on which the translations were built.

Later discoveries have vindicated the late Sir Frederic Kenyon (1863-1952), the well-known authority, when he stated:

'The Christian can take the whole Bible in his hand and say without fear or hesitation that he holds in it the true Word of God, handed down without essential loss from generation to generation throughout the centuries.'[1]

Moses talking Greek

Observant readers of the New Testament will have noticed that quotations from the Old Testament sometimes read differently from the Old Testament text. In many cases this is because the writer has quoted from the Greek translation, commonly called the Septuagint, or LXX. mentioned in Chapter 1.

There are some differences between the Hebrew text

and the LXX. Either the translators were working from a different Hebrew text from what descended to become the Masoretic, or they took liberties with the Hebrew as they had it. The former is the more generally accepted explanation, though there may have been some attempt to adapt slightly to a Greek readership. These details are of great interest to scholars, but the average reader may rest assured that no issues of salvation are at stake. Nor can we point to any manuscript and say that this is just what the prophet wrote to the letter and accents. During the Renaissance and Reformation there were Hebrew scholars who were able to go back to the Masoretic text, instead of relying on the Latin Vulgate. Notable were Tyndale in England, Martin Luther and J. Reuchlin (1455-1522) in Germany, for example.

Study continues to establish the soundest possible OT text, by careful comparison of manuscripts and versions and use of the increased knowledge of languages similar to biblical and of the customs of the times.[2]

The Greek Text of the New Testament

No manuscripts exist from the hands of New Testament writers or their scribes/amanuenses. We have at best copies of copies unto many generations. Copying by hand inevitably leads to errors. The eye can be deceptive, especially when some letters are alike, and when there is virtually no punctuation and no separation between words. The ear may also deceive. When a group of scribes took dictation, a number of Greek vowels were very similar in pronunciation, so the scribe wrote down what he decided was the meaning of what he heard. The mind could play tricks on a tired scribe.

Then there were intentional amendments made for various reasons: to 'improve' the Greek or to make the synoptic gospels, for example, harmonize more closely.

Alterations were made because of doctrinal considerations, either eliminating what was regarded as doctrinally unacceptable or inconvenient, for example the apparent contradiction between John 7:8 and 10, or introducing a scriptural 'proof' for a favourite theological tenet or practice (for example, fasting). An earlier scribe's marginal note (gloss) might be incorporated into the text, for a conscientious copier would not want to omit anything that might be the Word of God. Other additions were such details as the headings, 'The epistle of . . . ', and the subscriptions or colophons, for example, 'Written from Rome unto the Ephesians by Tychicus' at the end of Ephesians, which are marked off separately in the AV.[3]

There are numerous examples where similarity, either in spelling or in sound, between two words has introduced variant texts. For example *stolas* 'robes', *entolas*, 'commandments' in Revelation 2:14. Many other examples of textual differences could be cited to illustrate the point that there is nothing faith-shattering in the variations.

The result is that of the 5,000 or more Greek manuscripts, not any two agree in every detail. Yet, reassuringly, no book from ancient times is as well attested as the New Testament. The agreement is overwhelming; the differences are comparatively minor, and do not call into question any major doctrines of the Christian faith. No doctrine worthy of belief hangs on one proof text.

The Received Text or Textus Receptus (TR)

The fall of Constantinople to the Turks in 1453 accelerated an existing movement towards the study of Greek scholarship in the West, one of the factors contributing to the Renaissance. Now there was opportunity to study the New Testament in the original tongue rather than through the Vulgate.

Cardinal Francisco Ximenes de Cisneros (1437-1517), primate of Spain, prepared the Complutensian Polyglot with the New Testament in Greek and Latin. Although completed in 1514 it was not released until 1522. The underlying Greek manuscripts of this edition are unknown, although Ximenes expressed his indebtedness to Pope Leo X for the loan of 'very ancient codices'.[4]

Desiderius Erasmus (1469-1536), the best-known name in the Northern Renaissance, issued his Greek NT, based on late manuscripts, in 1516. Only one manuscript contained Revelation and even there chapter 22, verses 16-21 were missing, a gap among others which he filled by translating from the Vulgate back into Greek. 'In many places where it was not necessary, he "corrected" the Greek text to conform to the Latin'.[5] Suggestions that he had access to the Codex Vaticanus through a correspondent in Rome, but rejected it, are without any known foundation.

Erasmus provided the basis for the standard text for nearly 300 years, which was issued by Robert Stephanus in Paris in 1550, the first to divide into verses. Theodore Beza (1519-1605) issued ten editions, without moving far from Stephanus's text, although he had other MS evidence to hand. He faced the problem of how to cope with the differences between the Stephanus text and the Codex Bezae and other materials. In 1633 the brothers Bonaventura and Abraham Elzevir published an edition, based on Beza's work. The preface spoke of a received text, and this gave rise to the term Textus Receptus.

'Thus a text of the Greek NT which had been "edited" on the basis of late MS evidence and which too often had been "corrected" to the Latin text became stereotyped in man's minds. It was assumed for over three centuries to have some prescriptive right, just as if "an apostle had been the compositor".'[6]

Erasmus was a Catholic all his life, although not in sympathy with all that Rome did or taught. The late manuscripts Erasmus used were all from Catholic or Orthodox scriptoria.

Incidentally, we do not know the exact Greek text used by the AV translators. Explaining their reason for providing marginal readings, the AV translators wrote:

'They that are wise, had rather have their judgements at libertie in differences of readings, then to be captivated to one, when it may be the other.'[7]

The TR is not exactly the same as the Traditional or Majority Text. This fact will not be acceptable to those wedded to the exact words of the TR, but it was an issue faced by the conservative editors of the *New King James Version*, 1981.[8] The search for the best text did not stop with the Elzevir brother, as we shall see.

THIRTY-NINE AND TWENTY-SEVEN: SIXTY-SIX BOOKS IN ONE BIBLE

The canon of the Old Testament

The word 'canon', when used of the Bible, means the list of writings accepted as belonging to Jewish/Christian sacred scripture. By the time of Jesus there seems to have been general recognition by the Jewish people of what books were authoritative — the Law, the Prophets and the Writings — despite the fact that there were later discussions on some books. At Jamnia, AD 70-100, recognizing the growing distance between Judaism and Christianity, the Jewish elders were in general agreement on the thirty-nine books. The elders were concerned that the Jewish heritage was in danger from the tendency of some apocalyptic writing to weave together Jewish and non-Jewish beliefs. They did not accept into the canon the twelve books known collectively as the Apocrypha. The Christian Church accepted the Jewish OT canon without difficulty, but was inconsistent in its attitude to the Apocrypha. Some of the Fathers followed the Septuagint canon in not making a clear distinction between the thirty-nine and the twelve, while Origen, Cyril and Jerome held to the Jamnia canon. Although Jerome included the Apocrypha in his Latin translation, the Vulgate, he drew a distinction between the 'church books' (*libri ecclesiastici*) and the canonical books. The former could be read for edification, but not for confirmation of doctrine. Jerome's decision was highly influential. The twelve now form part of the Roman Catholic biblical canon. Some Protestants find the OT Apocrypha useful in understanding the period between the Testaments, though not treating them as valid sacred books.

The 1611 Authorized Version contained the OT Apocrypha, a point usually ignored by defenders of the AV. Perhaps it is a case of 'the times of this ignorance God winked at' (Acts 17:30). It was not until 1827 that the American Bible Society stopped printing the Apocrypha between the Old and New Testaments. The Trinitarian Bible Society in England was part of the same reaction against the twelve.

The canon of the New Testament

The early Church found itself under attack from those who claimed to have their own secret traditions handed down from Jesus or the apostles. Some claimed that Jesus had taught the apostles many things not mentioned in the gospels or the writings of Paul and others. The Church faced attacks from strange gospels, and from Gnosticism, a blend of pagan philosophy and fanciful notions in Christian dress. Essentially Gnosticism believed the material world to be fundamentally and hopelessly evil. For this reason Jesus Christ could not have been God in the flesh, truly God and man (John 1:14; 1 Tim. 3:16;

1 John 4:2, 3). The Church had to define its beliefs, and the basis of authority for those beliefs.

'I believe in . . . '

This led to the development of confessional statements or **creeds** (Latin *credo*, 'I believe'); to the idea of **church authority** (already foreshadowed in the letters to Timothy and Titus); and thirdly, what writings could be accepted as having authority, a **canon** (rule). It was the second century heretic, Marcion, who devised the first NT canon often Pauline epistles (minus the pastorals and Hebrews) and Luke's gospel, suitably edited to support his teaching. Marcion's selective use of Scripture made it imperative for the Church to define its own position. Some books — the Gospels, Acts and the Pauline epistles — were accepted almost from the time of writing. 2 Peter, 2 and 3 John, Jude, Hebrews and the Revelation took longer to gain acceptance. Attestations or quotations by the Fathers demonstrate the time of recognition of the various books. Some writings, the *Didache*, or *Teaching of the Twelve Apostles*, *The Shepherd of Hermas*, and *1 Clement*, hovered at the edges of acceptance for some time. The Council of Carthage (397) endorsed the sixty-six books generally accepted by Protestants.

Books that failed the test

There is also an Apocryphal New Testament, which is not accepted by any significant Christian communion. This was never a collection in the same way as the OT Apocrypha. The writings tended to imitate the various types of New Testament writing: gospels, acts, letters, and apocalypses (revelations). Several motives seem to have prompted this writing. First, the work of pious imagination. There was a desire to fill out the comparatively sparse information in the four gospels, for example on the first thirty years of Jesus' life. John had indicated that there was more to be said about the Lord's work and teaching if there were time and space enough (John 20:30; 21:25). Imagination went beyond the restrained style of the gospel accounts of miracle and wonder. There was also a desire to know more about what happened to the apostles, apart from what is recorded in Acts, and glimpses in the epistles.[9]

Secondly, the Gnostic writings sought to claim Jesus as their own. In recent years there have been discoveries of new Gnostic material, including the *Gospel of Thomas*, and these have interested scholars of Christian origins. Some even argue that Gnosticism was the original Christian faith, repressed by the dominant party. However, to read the NT apocrypha is to enter a different world from the twenty-seven books in the Bible. Joachim Jeremias and others have shown how the *Gospel of Thomas* gives a Gnostic twist to some episodes it shares with the canonical gospels, and misses the point of teaching recorded in the canonical books.[10] Tertullian (c.160/170– c.215/220) noted that truth precedes forgery. The apocryphal writings came later. There would have been no apocryphal work without the genuine preceding it. Forgery seeking to imitate or supplement writing inspired by the Holy Spirit is bound to show its uninspired origin.

The devout believer will see in the transmission of the canon a divine providence safeguarding the Bible, so that different Christian traditions, however much they may differ in aspects of faith and practice, work from the same New Testament, minor textual variations excepted.

---

[1] *Our Bible and the Ancient manuscripts*, London: Eyre and Spottiswoode, 5th edition, 1958, page 55.
[2] IDB 4:580-594.
[3] Bruce M. Metzger, *The Text of the New Testament. Its Transmission, Corruption and Restoration*, Oxford: Clarendon Press, 1964, pages 186-206.

[4]IDB 4:599.
[5]IDB 4:600.
[6]IDB 4:600.
[7]Opfell, page 159.
[8]Kubo, pages 291, 292.
[9]IDB 1:166-169; Supplementary Vol. pages 34-36. The NT Apocrypha is in print, but is not very profitable reading.
[10]*Parables*, pages 247-248, lists NT parables also found in Thomas.

CHAPTER SIX

The Greek text after 1611

Questioning the TR

Not the most interesting section, but foundations were being laid for modern developments.

The process of gathering and collating and comparing Greek and other MSS continued with the work of Brian Walton (1600-61), Dr John Fell (1625-86), John Mill (1645-1707), and Dr Edward Wells (1667-1727). Johann Albrecht Bengel (1687-1752), a German Pietist, was disturbed by the 30,000 variants in Mill's edition. Bengel established the criterion: 'the difficult is to be preferred to the easy (reading)'. He also divided the MSS into two families, the Alexandrian and the Constantinopolitan, or Byzantine as it would later be called. Bengel also wrote on Bible prophecy.

Johann Jakob Wettstein (1693-1754), a Swiss scholar, published his *Prolegomena* anonymously, since his textual views appeared to cast doubts on his orthodoxy in the climate of the time. The *Prolegomena* laid down nineteen principles for preparing an edition of the NT.

Johann Jakob Griesbach (1775-1812) carried forward the ideas of Bengel, Johann S. Semler (1725-91) and Wettstein, setting out fifteen canons of textual criticism. Bengel had divided the Greek MSS into two families: Griesbach divided the African family into two, and so proposed three families:

1. the Western, the text which had been in circulation in the early periods and had become corrupted through copyists' errors;

2. the Alexandrian, an attempt to revise the old corrupt text;

3. the Constantinopolitan, which flowed from the other two.[1]

Griesbach laid the foundations for the work of later scholars. Again it needs to be emphasized that 'criticism' does not mean negative, destructive attacks on the Word of God. Since no two extant MSS totally agree, even the most devout believer in biblical inerrancy has to make a choice between variants. Throughout the late eighteenth and nineteenth centuries, the number of MSS available increased, making possible a wider comparison of readings.

Karl Lachmann (1793-1851) was the first to break with the TR, publishing a different text in 1831. He set out to edit the Greek NT as if the *textus receptus* had never existed. Lachmann, Samuel Prideaux Tregelles (1813-75) and Constantin von Tischendorf (1815-74) all laid down principles for editing. Tregelles, a devout believer in the inspiration of Scripture, produced a Greek text based on the earliest witnesses.

The big two

Two manuscripts continue to play an important role in NT textual studies.

The Sinaiaticus (Aleph) was discovered by Tischendorf in 1844 in the Orthodox monastery of St Catherine on Mt Sinai. Parts of the MS had already been burned. Tischendorf found the remainder in a wastepaper basket. This hardly looks like a plot to subvert the faith of true Protestants. Aleph is a fourth century vellum manuscript, containing the Epistle of Barnabas and the Shepherd of Hermas in addition to the canonical NT books. Tischendorf discovered more MSS and printed more critical editions of the Greek NT than any other scholar. From 1869 to 1872, he worked on editing a

Greek text independent of the TR, using the Sinaiaticus (A) and Vaticanus (B) among other MSS.

The Vaticanus (B) (the very name itself is a provocation to ill-informed polemicists!) is an early fourth-century codex which once contained the whole Greek Bible. It was listed in the first Vatican Library catalogue 1475/1481, but was not released to scholars at that time, in fact not until 1864, a facsimile being issued in 1889-90,[2] so it could hardly have been used to 'suppress the Reformation', despite Jan Marcussen's assertions.[3] The Vatican is where the MS is housed; it is not more Roman Catholic for being kept in Rome than the Alexandrinus is Anglican for being kept in the British Museum. The Douai/Rheims Catholic English translation of 1582-1610 depended on the Vulgate, not the Vaticanus, as did Ronald Knox's translation of 1950. It has been suggested that Vaticanus was one of the fifty copies ordered by Constantine, AD 331, but other signs point to Egypt as its birthplace. It is of undoubted antiquity, although antiquity alone is not proof of textual purity.

Westcott and Hort

What has been said above illustrates the fact that investigation into Greek MSS had been in progress long before the work of Brook Foss Westcott (1825-1901) and F. J. A. Hort (1828-92). In view of outrageous attacks on these scholars made by some misguided zealots, it may be worth letting Westcott speak:

'A corrupted Bible is a sign of a corrupted Church, a Bible mutilated or imperfect, a sign of a Church not yet raised to the complete perception of Truth. . . . We might have thought that a Bible of which every part should bear a visible and unquestioned authentification of its divine origin, separated by a solemn act from the first from the . . . fate of all other literature, would have best answered our concepts of what the written records of revelation should be. But it is not thus that God works among us. In the Church and in the Bible alike, He works through men. As we follow the progress of their formation, each step seems truly human, and when we contemplate the whole, we joyfully recognize that every part is also divine.'[4]

This Cambridge duo developed and applied the genealogical and other principles for the evaluation of MSS.[5] They divided the known Greek MSS into families, groups of texts showing the greatest similarity. They believed that one of the various families could be shown to be the earliest and best, and its readings in general would be preferred on that basis. Rules of criticism were employed to determine which family was nearest to the autographs, the original from the hand of the NT writer: a shorter reading is to be preferred to a longer, the choice of the variant reading which would best explain the origin of all the other variants in the passage, and the acceptance of the reading which appeared to be most in harmony with the author's thought and style.

Four families of text

Westcott and Hort believed there were four families of text:

1. Western, with its love of paraphrase and expansion, which included Codex Bezae, the Old Syrian, and the Old Latin;

2. Alexandrian, comprising a small group of MSS supposedly from Egypt, a classification of certain readings found in the other three families;

3. Syrian/Byzantine, represented by the great majority of Greek NT MSS, both uncials and minuscules. They considered this to be the latest, a conflation of the three other families. Little importance was attached to this family, to which the TR belonged;

4. Neutral, which was exemplified by codex Vaticanus (B) and codex Sinaiaticus (Aleph), and found in Origen. This Neutral text they believed to be a composite, a conflation of the three other families, and the closest to the autographs. The TR was almost totally rejected. As M. M. Parvis put it, they 'finally dealt the death blow to the *textus receptus*, but in doing so they set up what has come to be a new *textus receptus* and "canonized" a new method for textual studies, the genealogical method'.[6]

The publication of the Revised Version in 1881, based largely on the text of Westcott and Hort, brought the new biblical scholarship out of the confines of the scholarly world to public attention, both friendly and hostile.

Since Westcott and Hort, further discoveries and study have co-operated to shake confidence in the exclusive predominance assigned by them to the Vaticanus and Sinaiaticus text.[7]

Today we may distinguish four types or families, similar to the Westcott and Hort categories:

1. Western, mainly Codex Bezae and Old Latin. Bezae contains a remarkable addition after Luke 6:5, apparently inserted to promote working on the Sabbath;

2. Caesarean, used in Egypt and Palestine as early as the second century;

3. Byzantine, the basis of the Textus Receptus, the Received Text of the AV;

4. Alexandrian. Confusingly, this is not what Westcott and Hort meant by the term, but what they called the Neutral text;

Some authorities add a fifth, Syriac, the text of the Old Syriac gospels. Not to be confused with the Westcott and Hort Syrian text.

Manuscripts – unfinished business

The search still continues to establish the best possible

manuscript evidence for the text of the Bible, especially the New Testament. The evidence is found in various forms:

1. Pottery or limestone fragments (ostraca);

2. Papyrus;

3. Uncials, based on capital letters, written on vellum or parchment, into the ninth century;

4. Minuscules, a cursive or running hand ninth to seventeenth, or eighteenth centuries, written on vellum or parchment;

5. Lectionaries, or service books, containing the scripture readings, or lessons, for the day;

6. Versions, the most significant of which were made before AD 1000. They include Latin, Syriac, Coptic, Armenian, Old Slavic and Gothic;

7. Quotations of scripture in the Church Fathers.

Since Westcott and Hort it has become clear that the genealogical method is not adequate to determine the original text. Textual criticism is more eclectic than in the past. The preferred reading is considered to be that which best fits the style of the author, and which best explains the origin of all other variants.

Criteria for deciding between variant readings

First, the shorter reading is to be preferred, for the reason that a scribe was more likely to add to a text than to omit. Of course, where the eye has clearly skipped a line, or made an obvious omission, this rule would not apply.

Secondly, the harder reading is to be preferred as a scribe was more likely to simplify a statement to make it easier to understand than to introduce difficulty.

Thirdly, the characteristic style of the writer has to be considered. The story of the woman taken in adultery (John 8:1-11) is not in John's style and seems unlikely to have been his writing. The earliest MSS do not contain it. However, the episode has 'the ring of truth', and Jerome included it in the Vulgate. Its authenticity as a story of Jesus' ministry is generally accepted, at least by evangelicals. If we regard it as a tradition which has some-how been misplaced, we do not weaken its authority. After all, it is clear that the order of events is not the first essential for gospel writers, otherwise the gospels would be more uniform.

Seeking the true text

A scholar who sets out to establish the true biblical text will have an underlying set of beliefs about Scripture. The work of Origen, the first 'textual critic', was based on three major beliefs: Church tradition is the framework within which the scholar must work; scripture is a unity and God gave light equally in both the OT and NT; all scripture is inspired, so that whether every part of it looks important to the reader or not is important, and is to be interpreted in such a way that God is not dishonoured. His regard for the tradition of the Church made him reluctant to change copies of the NT in actual use. Some of Origen's speculations were extravagant beyond the bounds of orthodoxy. His devotion to the biblical text is undoubted, but unguarded statements laid him open to suspicion even in his own day.[8]

Early printed editions of the NT (that is, Cardinal Ximenes, Erasmus, Stephanus, the Elzevirs, Beza and others) largely depended on late Greek MSS used uncritically. Stephanus placed variant readings in the margin, but incurred such fierce criticism that he fled Paris for safety in Geneva.

Dean John W. Burgon's attacks on the RV and the work of Westcott and Hort will be considered in Chapter 8. It is important to realize that New Testament textual studies have moved on since the 1880s. Their methods are not applied thoughtlessly.

The situation today

Neither the Westcott and Hort methodology nor their text are as dominant today as some writers claim, the preference being for an eclectic approach.[9] The weight of conservative biblical scholarship favours the readings of the uncials, B and Aleph, but not rigidly, especially as they differ up to 3,000 times in the gospels alone, according to Pickering.[10] Philip Wesley Comfort believes that modern textual criticism has moved too far in the direction of subjectivism and internal evidence in the making of text-critical decisions, arguing for a return to the more objective principles of Westcott and Hort.[11]

Omissions

'For there are three that bear record in heaven, the Father, the Word, and the Holy Ghost: and these three are one.' (1 John 5:7.) Most conservative scholars recognize that this verse is a gloss (marginal comment), not found in any Greek MS before the fifteenth century, and even this seems to have been 'custom-made' to force Erasmus to keep his promise that if he found just one MS with that verse he would include it in his text. The doctrine of the Holy Trinity does not depend on maybe the pious gloss of a scribe who wanted to expand on the threefold witness of 1 John 5:8. Good causes are not helped by unsound arguments.[12] There may be stronger evidence for the passage than was known in Erasmus' day, but to discuss this would take too much space here.

Readers of some modern translations will be faced with a question on Mark 16:9-20. There are four different extant endings to Mark's gospel, although only two merit serious consideration. Did Mark actually end at verse 8?

Conservative scholars believe the best attested of the four is the version which appears in the TR. Whatever ending is accepted it is clear that there is some stylistic difference between the long ending and the rest of the gospel, though advocates of the traditional long ending make a case for similarities.[13] It is certainly unlikely that Mark would have deliberately ended his book at verse 8, although some scholars believe this. Would a story which began in such breathless triumph end in fear? Was he interrupted, or was the last page of the codex somehow lost? Should the matter be settled solely on the basis of textual evidence, or should theological judgement enter in?

The tough rebuke to the disciples (verse 14) and what some have seen as 'the bizarre promise of immunity from snakes and poisonous drinks . . . completely out of character with the person of Christ', have led some scholars to question verses 9-20 on theological as well as textual grounds.[14] But elsewhere our Lord used hyperbole, and Paul was later to shake off a viper. We may note in passing that Mark 16:9-20 introduces no concepts not found in the other gospels, except the problematic verse 18, though even here Luke 10:18 offers some parallels.

G. D. Fee discusses the difficult verses John 5:3b-4, not found in many MSS. As he points out, there 'is a kind of capriciousness to "grace" that allows only one to be healed, and only the first into the pool at that'.[15] The one who least needed healing would be most able to obtain it. However, it is dangerous to seek to eliminate texts that may be theologically inconvenient, and Fee's argument is based on textual grounds, not on theological.

Some of the changes in the traditional text are:

The omission of 'For thine is the kingdom . . . Amen' from Matthew 6:13.

The eunuch's confession, 'I believe that Jesus Christ is

the Son of God,' (Acts 8:37) is omitted from some modern translations.

' . . . of his flesh, and of his bones' is sometimes missed out from Ephesians 5:30.

Revelation 22:14 usually appears in modern translations as 'wash their robes', not 'keep his commandments'.

An incarnation 'proof text', where the AV reads 'God was manifested' is variously translated as 'He', 'Who', or 'Which'.[16] This is not an attempt to weaken the text, but to be true to the Greek which actually uses a pronoun, not the word God in the most ancient MSS. However, reading the verse in context makes it clear what Paul meant.

Jesus' opponents scornfully told Nicodemus to do his homework, for 'no prophet is to rise from Galilee' (John 7:52, RSV). They were not correct for there had been prophets from the north. A single letter changed would give the reading 'the prophet, that is, Messiah, does not arise from Galilee', and one very ancient MS has this reading. Not an important point, but it shows how manuscript discoveries can open up new understanding.[17]

At this point the reader may well ask what significance this has for the ordinary Christian who reads the Bible for devotion. The changes between the AV and the RV, reflecting the underlying MSS are minor, both in the Old Testament and the New. Carson, with a high view of inspiration, believes that reverent biblical textual scholarship results in a 'sure and certain word from God'.[18]

---

[1]IDB 4:607.

[2]Metzger, 1964, page 47.

[3]Jan Marcussen, '20 Theses against the New International Version, and other new perversions of the Bible based on "Roman Catholic" and "Sinaiaticus", and upholding the King James Version as the Holy Word of God.' xc, PO Box 68, Thompsonville, IL 62890.

[4]Preface to *The Bible in the Church*, 1884 in IDB 4:608-609.

[5]Metzger 1964, pages 129-131.

[6]IDB 4:608.

[7]For later developments in textual studies, Metzger 64, pages 137-146.

[8]IDB 4:603.

[9]E. J. Epp and G. D. Fee, *Studies in the Theory and Method of New Testament Criticism*, Grand Rapids, MI: Eerdmans, 1993, pages 12-16.

[10]G. W. Anderson, *The Greek New Testament*, London: TBS, 1994, page 3.

[11]*The Quest for the Original Text of the New Testament*, Grand Rapids, MI: Baker Book House, 1992.

[12]D. A. Carson, *The King James Version Debate*, Grand Rapids, MI: Baker Book House, 1979, pages 34, 35, 59-61; Metzger 1964, pages 101, 102; for a brief sober defence of the verses, G. W. and D. E. Anderson, *Why 1 John 5:7, 8 is in the Bible*, London: TBS, 1993.

[13]W. W. Wessell in *EDC 8*, pages 791-793; *The Authenticity of the Last Twelve Verses of the Gospel According to Mark*, London, TBS, anon, nd.

[14]quoted in *EBC 8*, page 793.

[15]G. D. Fee 'On the authenticity of John 5:3b-4', *Evangelical Quarterly*, 54 (1982), page 218.

[16]*God was manifested in the flesh (1 Timothy 3:16)*, London: TBS, anon, nd, is a short defence of the AV rendering.

[17]Nida, pages 201, 202.

[18]Carson, *Debate*, page 24.

CHAPTER SEVEN

The Authorized Version

The 'inspired' translation

Is the Authorized Version an 'inspired' translation? Does it have authority in its own right, almost regardless of the underlying Greek text? Wyclif (1382), Tyndale (1525), Coverdale (1535), Matthew (1537), the Great Bible (1540), the Geneva Bible (1560), and the Bishops' Bible (1568), were forerunners of the AV (1611). About nine-tenths of William Tyndale's language was incorporated into the AV.

Despite, or because of royal patronage and the florid address to James I, the AV was not an instant success. There was a natural desire to keep to the familiar. The Geneva Bible, with its distinctively 'Protestant' marginal notes of increasing degrees of radicalism with each successive version, was beloved of those of a puritan bent who resisted the catholicizing trends they believed they detected in James and Charles I. Forgotten today even by most of those who are its spiritual heirs, the Geneva Bible 'became the Elizabethan best seller, the set book of the Scottish Reformation, the guide book for the English navigators, the companion of those pilgrims who went into "the howling wilderness" of Massachusetts.'[1]

Not everyone liked it

The Pilgrim Fathers refused to have the AV aboard the *Mayflower*, clinging to their Geneva Bibles. This might surprise their descendants who vociferously defend the AV (Wilkinson insists they carried the 1611 version with them, page 256).

Not only Puritans disliked the AV. Hugh Broughton,

(1549-1612), a noted scholar, perhaps prejudiced because he was not selected as a translator, wrote, 'The new edition crosseth me. I require it to be burnt.'[2]

Revising the AV

The 1611 text was itself revised in 1613, 1629, 1675, 1762 and 1769, and of course, the *New King James Version* (1982). The *Revised Version* of 1881, the *American Standard Version* (1901) and the *Revised Standard Version* (1952) are basically revisions of the AV rather than new translations.

What the translators said

The dedication to King James I is printed in most AV Bibles. What is not so commonly known is the preface, 'The Translators to the Readers'. Several points emerge from this preface, if we are prepared to listen carefully to King James's men.

First, they expected opposition and they got it. Secondly, they had a high view of Scripture, and the need for it to be available in the language of the people. They noted the work of compilers, such as Origen and Epiphanius, who worked on the Greek Old Testament. They praised Jerome, 'the best Linguist . . . of his age' for his Latin Vulgate. They recognized that the Puritan party at the Hampton Court Conference had urged the need of a new translation. They realized that 'some imperfections and blemishes' will appear in a translation, but it is still the Word of God. The New Testament writers used the Septuagint Greek translation of the Old Testament, even though it differs from the original in many places, 'neither doth it come neer it, for perspecuitie, gravitie, majestie'. Some readers would prefer not to have marginal readings, but the translators believed these to be helpful. In God's providence there are some words of doubtful meaning, 'not in doctrinall points that concern salvation (for in such it hath been vouched that the Scriptures are plain). . . .'[3]

The nearly fifty translators were of course all clergy of the Church of England, *with very few Puritans among them*. The 1611 men did not plan that one English word should consistently stand for a word in the original. 'For is the kingdome of God become words and syllables? Why should we be in bondage to them if we may be free? use one precisely, when we may use another no less fit as commodiously.' For example, in Romans 5 the same Greek word is variously translated rejoice (verse 2), glory (verse 2) and joy (verse 11). The RSV uses 'rejoice' throughout. If one is talking of wooden faithfulness to the Greek, who did better, the men of 1611 or 1881? Both received a great deal of flak for their pains!

Difficulties today

There are several difficulties in the AV for the modern reader. First, the many changes of word meanings since 1611. The language was hardly contemporary at that time. Those who have grown up with the AV may not recognize the difficulties of those who come new to the text. Some of these issues were discussed earlier.

Secondly, is the fact that from modern discoveries of secular documents we know much more about *Koine* Greek, the language of the New Testament, than in 1611. This means a more accurate translation can be made, even if the Greek text of the AV is retained.

Thirdly, it would be wrong to assume that every word in the AV as we have it is a good translation of the original. No Christian doctrine may legitimately depend on how translators have rendered Hebrew or Greek into English. Those who claim virtual inerrancy for the AV need to recognize that their case is not so simple as they suggest.

The word 'God' is not in the Greek *me genoito*, translated as 'God forbid' in the AV (Rom. 3:4; 1 Cor. 6:15).

The translators used an English idiom to convey Paul's thought. Vulture, that hovering undertaker 'preoccupied with sepulture', is a more likely translation than eagle in Luke 17:37. The Greek can be translated either way.

Different in Greek, same in English

The AV does not distinguish between the two words translated 'love' and the two words both rendered as 'feed' (John 21:15-17). Those with a high regard for accuracy will ponder on the reason for John's use of different words in Greek, although John is given to variation. The two words, 'feed' and 'tend' bring out two aspects of the shepherd's work. Peter remembered the figure of the Shepherd (1 Peter 2:25; 5:4).

What are non-episcopalians to do with the word 'bishop' (*episkopos*), if we are to hold to the absolute authority of every word of the AV to the effect that every word must mean what the 1611 translators meant?

Translating both *hades* and *gehenna* as hell seems to assume that they mean the same, and refer to the everlasting place (of torment?) of the damned. The meaning of these words, and *sheol* in the Old Testament need careful individual study.

The literal translation, referring to the Holy Spirit as 'itself', seems strange to the reader attuned to the personality of the Third Person (Rom. 8:26).

'He is guilty of death' is a mistranslation of the Greek taken from the Catholic Douai-Rheims version. The meaning is 'He is liable to/deserves death' (Matt. 26:66; cf. Luke 23:15). The 1611 'shamefastness' was changed fifty years later by a (mysogonistic?) printer's error to 'shamefacedness' and has remained ever since, as if that expressed Paul's idea. 'I beheld till the thrones were cast down' means not an overthrowing but as the NIV says, '"As I looked, thrones were set in place"' (Daniel 7:9). In other words, the court room scene is prepared.

New light on old words

Study of secular examples of the language in which the NT was written sometimes give new or enhanced meanings for biblical words. Did Paul say 'give in marriage' (AV), or marry? Papyri discovered after 1611 showed that *gamizo* may be translated either way, according to context. The interpreter/translator's understanding of the meaning of 'virgin' (*parthenos*), variously understood as unmarried daughter, spiritual bride/companion in chastity, and fiancée, will be influenced by both the meaning of *gamizo*, and by possible theological concepts regarding the superiority of the unmarried state (1 Cor. 7:36-38).[4]

Why keep the AV?

Various reasons are given for clinging to the Authorized Version, and there are some who urge that nothing else is acceptable.

First, the AV is unique, as George Bernard Shaw rather surprisingly wrote:

'The translation was extraordinarily well done because to the translators what they were translating was not merely a curious collection of ancient books written by different authors in different stages of culture, but the Word of God divinely revealed through His chosen and expressly inspired scribes. In this conviction they carried out their work with boundless reverence and care and achieved a beautifully artistic result.'[5]

William Lyon Phelps declared:

'We have the best Bible in the world . . . the most beautiful monument erected with the English alphabet . . . an incomparably rich inheritance. . . . This means we ought . . . to use the AV: all others are inferior.'[6]

Secondly, the AV has led people to salvation over the centuries, and it is part of the English-speaking heritage. Its beauty is unsurpassed, and this is the version that at least the older generation memorized.

Some argue that if there is a multiplicity of translations, listeners in church are confused, and people will not memorize any version. Verrecchia (noted in Chapter One) was not against memorization and familiarity as such, but against the danger of the memory shielding us from the impact of the message.

Then there are suspicions that any changes in the wording of the AV will result in theological loss. The translators may not deal faithfully with the original language. While this is a legitimate concern, it can become stolid and mere obstinacy if no word can be changed from the AV, however obscure the meaning has become to the modern reader. The NKJV is an attempt to keep the substance of the AV, while making it more intelligible.

Loving and trusting the AV

Those who advocate new translations in English must recognize the strength of feeling of those who love the AV. The Trinitarian Bible Society, founded in 1831, circulates 'the Canonical books WITHOUT NOTE OR COMMENT, to the exclusion of the Apocrypha; copies in the English language shall be those of the Authorised Version'.[7] The society uses the Masoretic text of the Old Testament and the Received Greek text for the New (See chapter 5). The balanced statement of the TBS is worth quoting:

'While perfection is not claimed for the Authorized Version . . . , or for any other version, it is known that the translators of the Authorized Version acknowledged the Divine inspiration, authority and inerrancy of the Holy Scriptures. . . . It is the most accurate and trustworthy translation into English available, and is the only English version published by the Society.'[8]

While this writer may not agree with everything in that paragraph, the sincerity must be admired. No one will be lost by following the TBS principles. However, the statement does seem to imply that translators other than the 1611 men may not have held such a high view of biblical inspirationists. While that may be true of some, the clearly-expressed views of other translators and scholars indicate a doctrine of inspiration on a level with that of the AV fifty. A reading of their Preface makes it clear that they were not verbal inspirationists in the rigid sense that they believed the originals before them were free of variants and ambiguities.

However, any doctrine that depends on a particular translation alone for its proof texts is unfit to be called a Bible doctrine. Beliefs must be based on what the original languages say, and in most translations a clear consensus emerges.

The Word of God was not and is not bound to any one language, time or culture, although it is of course rooted in a culture (2 Timothy 2:9).

---

[1]Maurice S. Betteridge, 'The Bitter Notes: The Geneva Bible and its Annotations'. *The Sixteenth Century Journal*, XLV.1 (Spring 1983) 41-62 (62).

[2]F. F. Bruce, *History of the Bible in English*, Guildford: Lutterworth, 1979, page 107.

[3]Opfell, pages 149, 159, 160.

[4]Beegle, pages 90, 91.

[5]Cited in the Preface to the New King James Version, page iii.

[6]Cited in Wilkinson, page 90.

[7]*The Trinitarian Bible Society, The Constitution of the TBS*, London: TBS, 1992, para 3.
[8]TBS, *Introduction*, np.

CHAPTER EIGHT

Defenders of tradition

Criticisms of modern translations

'And certain men which came down from Judea taught the brethren and said, Except ye use the Authorized King James Version ye cannot be saved.' (With apologies to Acts 15:1.)

Text and translation

There are two criteria in assessing a translation: the best possible Hebrew/Aramaic/Greek text, and a faithful rendering of the meaning into the receptor tongue, aided by the Holy Spirit.

There is a vocal section of Christian writers who attack anything that is not the AV on the twin grounds of text and translation. To give some special inspirational status on either of these grounds to the men of 1611 is far beyond what they would have wished if we read their preface. One fundamentalist group even urges its Scandinavian followers to use the AV, even when their knowledge of English is limited. This is to pass from Bible loving to bibliolatry. It is difficult for some who cannot read or speak any other language than English to realize that valid and trustworthy Bible translations can exist outside their monolingual boundaries. In the play *St Joan*, an English priest asks whether Joan's voices spoke in French or English. If in French the voices were obviously from the devil. English voices might be from on high. Of course, George Bernard Shaw is having a little fun, but there is an element of truth, as in all effective satire. The heavy emphasis on the need to adhere to the words of the AV suggests an Anglo-centred view of the world. The

Anglo-Saxons have claimed a special place in God's plans, from the days of John Foxe, Bishop Jewell ('God is English'), the Solemn League and Covenant, John Milton, and then America, the 'Redeemer Nation' with its 'manifest destiny'. The fresh innocence of a Foxe or Jewell can develop into the terrible Hegelian destiny to be achieved by the nation-state or the class struggle, or the fantasies of British Israelism which even now fuel some of the Militia groups of the USA.

The view from Paris

It can be an eye-opener to step outside the Anglo-Saxon perspective. Just as there are some who believe, we are told, that the English Bible was good enough for the apostle Paul, so apparently, there are those who believe 'that God Himself wrote it in French and sent it down complete from heaven'.[1] Luther's German Bible (1534), probably more influential in its sphere than the AV, is no longer contemporary German, and there are modern translations. So we could go through a long list of European languages.

What's wrong?

Duthie lists a number of reasons given for condemning a version:
• Disagreement with the author's religious belief, regardless of whether these are reflected in the translation.
• The Greek TR or 'Majority' text was not used.
• The level of English.
• Divine pronouns are not capitalized, ignoring the fact that the AV does not do so. The fashion seems to have been an aspect of nineteenth-century piety.
• The version does not have 'Holy' in the title.[2]

Translate every word?

In considering types of translation, we have already looked at the argument that every WORD must be translated, and nothing added. In this respect the Douai/ Rheims was more strict than the AV. Strict defenders of the AV need to look again at the number of words in italics, in other words, words supplied by the translator in order to make the meaning clearer. 'Now a certain (man) was sick (named) Lazarus.' (John 11:1.) The words 'as though he heard them not' are not found in the TR, and seem to have been inserted as a comment on Jesus' silence (John 8:6). This insertion would, one suspects, have been eagerly pounced upon had it been perpetrated by a modern translator. The TR reads 'And passing along he saw . . . .' (John 9:1.) The AV recasts the sentence and inserts the word Jesus for clarity. If a modern translator, even using the TR omits the name Jesus, it is not theological bias, but faithfulness to the original.

Strict faithfulness to the words of the original also involves the question of whether theological terms such as repentance, redemption, sanctification should be translated by one English word or expanded to give the meaning. The difficulty for many English readers today is that they do not have the background to understand what these abstract nouns mean.

John W. Burgon

It is time to look at the defenders of the AV and the TR, beginning with John W. Burgon, *The Revised Version*.[3] Burgon has little but scorn for the Revised Version and its translators. He set the pattern for later critics of new versions by attacking both deviations from the TR and the changes in English even where the text itself is not in dispute. He also set the tone for many later detractors by his invective and his indignation that, in addition to representation from Presbyterians, Wesleyans, and Congregationalists, a Socinian (anti-Trintarian, rationalist) was on the translating team and had been allowed to take communion in Westminster Abbey.

In a work of such length and detail it is not surprising that he sometimes made some palpable hits at the scholarship and felicity of the Revised Version. To some extent Burgon was attacking a windmill, since the Revised Version never supplanted the AV in popular affection and general usage. However, he provided a quarry for most of the defenders of the AV and opponents of new versions.

Burgon the scholar

Burgon was no mean scholar. Prejudiced he may have been, but he was not blind. He did not hold to the infallibility of the TR. He freely granted that here and there 'the orthodox themselves may have sought to prop up truths which the early heretics most perseveringly assailed'.[4] His quarrel was with what he saw as the tyranny established by the Codex Sinaiaticus (Aleph) and the Vaticanus (B).[5] He blamed Marcion, the early Gnostic, for the 'mutilated form' of the Lord's prayer in Luke 11, and in Matthew 6:13b.[6] Despite the substantial differences in the readings of these codices, a factor which Burgon exploited heavily, he saw a 'sinister resemblance' which he put down to their both being derived from a corrupt common source. So what reinforces their authenticity for Westcott and Hort, is an indication of their corruption for Burgon. He wrote colourfully. Manuscripts he disliked are described as 'scandalously corrupt', 'depraved', 'mutilated'.

For Burgon there were three sources: the large number of Copies, the Versions, and Patristic Citations. He argued that these sources had not been properly explored and evaluated by the revisers. Changes in the text, he argued, came mainly from four different causes: Copyists' errors, Design, Assimilation, and Mutilation. Examples of the second are a 'pious insertion' in some MSS of a promise to return the colt (Luke 19:33), and the rationalistic change from 'eclipse' to 'darkened' (Luke 23:45). Mutilation is intentional as opposed to accidental omission. An example is the omission of 'second Sabbath after the first' (Luke 6:1), which removes a chronological conundrum. Other mutilations may have been made for more sinister reasons, 'derogating the Lord's majesty'.[7]

Burgon's influence lives on in the continuing arguments against modern translations since they rely heavily on unreliable manuscripts, notably the Vaticanus (B) and the Sinaiaticus (Aleph). The story of the Greek text was told in Chapter 5.

The deity and virgin birth of Jesus Christ

Among the charges levelled at new translations is that the deity of Christ is undermined, and this is a genuine concern to level-headed defenders of the AV. Selective evidence can be made to demonstrate this point, but the whole picture must be examined. The AV, following the TR, reads 'the God and the Father of our Lord Jesus Christ' (Col. 1:3). The RV and most modern translations omit the 'and'. This omission actually *strengthens* the force of Paul's affirmation of Christ's deity by removing any possible ambiguity that a quibbler might introduce by suggesting that God and the Father were two different persons. Victor Perry examined eight texts, not including Colossians 1:3, in ten translations, with marginal readings in five of these, making fifteen variants, where the text may state that Jesus is God. He found four instances in the AV, six in the RV, four in the NEB, five in the TEV, seven in the NIV. As expected, there were none in the New World Translation, which reflects the Jehovah's

Witnesses' understanding of Christ. The NIV calls Jesus 'God' in John 1:1; Titus 2:13; 2 Peter 1:1 where the AV does not, although the NIV margin omits 'God' from John 1:18; Acts 20:28; Romans 9:5.[8] Critics compile very complete lists of what they consider to be deletions from the TR. Very seldom are additions noted in the direction of orthodoxy.

The change from 'Joseph' to 'father' in newer translations appears to some to undermine the virgin birth (Luke 2:33). It is quite unthinkable that Catholics would alter a text in this direction. Mary's statement at the Annunciation is clear in modern versions, and also the words 'the son (as was supposed) of Joseph' (Luke 1:34; 3:23).

'Only begotten'
The omission of 'begotten', *monogenes*, from translations of its five occurrences in John's writing is taken by some as a further attack on the deity of Jesus. The Greek *monogenes* is used nine times in the NT. Of these, five refer to Jesus, all in John's writing, to the son of the widow of Nain, to Jairus' daughter, the demoniac son and Isaac (Luke 7:12; 8:42; 9:38; Heb. 11:17). In the LXX, *monogenes* is used for 'only'. Tyndale omitted the word. The AV rendering of *monogenes* for Jesus is 'the only begotten Son', a translation of Jerome's *unigenitus*, influenced by the Nicene Creed (AD 325). Previous Latin versions had used *unicus*, 'only' or 'only one', 'unique'. So we find the Catholic Jerome actually strengthening the emphasis on the uniqueness of Jesus, going beyond the Greek, perhaps resonating with Psalm 2:7 and Hebrews 1:5; 5:5. 'Begotten' adds nothing to the understanding of the deity of our Lord, nor does its omission detract. The Apostles' Creed reads 'Jesus Christ His only (*monogenes*) Son'.

We have the paradox of fundamentalist Protestants

arguing for a translation based on the Latin of a Catholic translation.[9] The translation 'one and only' (John 3:16, NIV) accurately renders the Greek and does not detract from the deity of our Lord, despite Riplinger's assertion.[10] The term 'begotten' is unclear to those unversed in the Trinitarian controversies of the early Church, and it would be interesting to ask those who argue vehemently against its omission what they understand by it. The true voice (*ipsissima vox*) of Scripture is not tied to the exact words (*ipsissima verba*) of the AV.

Son of God, sons of God

Richard Longenecker points out that the problem of translating monogenes is paralleled by the issue of *huios* (son), *huios theou* (Son of God) and the plural form, used to refer to Christians. John always reserved the 'Son' and 'Son of God' for Jesus. John, the last of the New Testament writers, has a more deeply developed Christology than the synoptic writers. In his use of *monogenes*, John was emphasizing Christ's unique quality, *huios* stressed the divine nature, the deity.

'We must conclude . . . that the translation "only begotten Son", though venerable, fails to capture adequately John's point of view in his use of *monogenes huios* (or *monogenes theos* in John 1:18), particularly because it leaves open the possibility of an etymological emphasis on *genes* (the idea of generation), because it neglects then current usage for the word, and because it fails to set the determination of meaning in the context of John's avowedly heightened christological perspective.'[11]

The key word in the hymn on the deity of Jesus Christ, 1 Timothy 3:16, is either 'He' (most versions) or 'God', as in the AV. Burgon explains the change as scribal error,[12] and this is the standard defence of the TR reading today.

Conservatism, fundamentalism and the AV

This recent revival of advocacy of the TR and the AV may be seen as another manifestation of popular fundamentalism. In the arguments of the ranters, the AV wording and the TR are almost inextricably mixed up, but more scholarly work is concentrated on the defence of the TR, recognizing that no translation is perfect. Terence Brown of the Trinitarian Bible Society, David Otis Fuller, Zane Hodges and Wilbur N. Pickering, both of Dallas Theological Seminary have in recent years attempted a reasoned defence of the TR. To be exact, these scholars argue for the Majority text, the so-called Byzantine, rather than for every jot and tittle of the TR. Pickering's 179 pages offer perhaps the most cogent recent arguments, first by seeking to discredit the Westcott and Hort method, though not the men, and presenting the case for the Byzantine text.[13] He is successful in showing that reliance on the W-H theories lives on even though they have been somewhat discredited. One is reminded of the way in which the name Darwin is invoked, even though some of his conclusions are no longer considered valid. The arguments for the TR, and consequently the AV are briefly set out in pamphlets by G. W. and D. E. Anderson, published by the Trinitarian Bible Society. This is the standard repertoire, made accessible for people in a hurry, but based on serious work.

Gordon D. Fee and D. A. Carson have both written critiques of Pickering.[14] Fee argues that Pickering misunderstands (1) text critical methodology; (2) the causes of textual corruption; (3) the correct use of the Church Fathers. Pickering's concern is theological, not merely academic. After having demolished W-H, to his own satisfaction, Pickering argued that the large number of MSS offer independent witness to the original text, and secondly, that most of the corruption to the NT text was deliberate, theologically motivated. The case for the Byzantine text, in the current state of scholarship, really hangs on the validity of Pickering's case.

D. A. Carson sets out his own demolition job on the supreme authority of the Byzantine text in general and the TR in particular in 'Fourteen Theses'.[15] He first points out that defenders of the TR are quoted, but the work of B. B. Warfield and J. Gresham Machen, first-class evangelical scholars, is ignored. The difficulty for the reader of defences of the TR is that every omission and variation from the TR is listed, but seldom is anything said when the evidence goes the other way, and the Nestle/Aland or other critical texts (in the strict scholarly sense) have readings which strengthen theological beliefs they hold dear.

Work in progress

Pickering ended on a note of optimism, believing that 'in terms of closeness to the original, the King James Version and the *Textus Receptus* have been the best available up to now'. However, he looked forward to computer-assisted comparison of 4,500 MSS on microfilm which would lead to a definitive text, 'the full and final story'.[16] This openness on Pickering's part is refreshing when compared with those for whom there is nothing beyond the true word of the TR and AV. Carson points out that the very diversity of readings among examples of the Byzantine text makes a rigid defence of the TR untenable. 'In about a dozen places its reading is attested by **no known Greek manuscript** witness.'[17] The issue here is not the quality of manuscript evidence, but the absence of any in these cases.

Beyond the fringe

Sometimes a critic who ought to know better sacrifices

scholarship to prejudice. B. F. Wilkinson dramatically heads a paragraph 'a deadly blow against miracles', when the translation 'signs' is used in John. One might think that he is protesting against critics who deny or rationalize Jesus' work. Unfortunately for Wilkinson, John wrote, 'sign' (*semeia*), whereas Matthew, Mark and Luke spoke of miracle (*dunamis*). The AV translators used 'miracle' for both words in many instances. Wilkinson's quarrel is really with John for not using the 'right' word. John in reply might say that, guided by the Holy Spirit, he used 'signs' for a good reason. This seems to be an instance where a defender of the AV seems prepared to stick to the English text regardless of the Greek.[18]

The Latin Vulgate, the Bible in the language of the time

Wilkinson praises the Old Latin Versions, although it is most unlikely he ever read them. He asserts that the Papacy required an 'Origenistic Bible', and this Jerome was commissioned to produce.[19] Origen, with his wide-ranging speculations, beyond the bounds of orthodoxy, is an easy target. Pickering, as we have seen, a strong defender of the Received Text and AV points out, as part of his argument, that from the third century the text was so well known that 'even an Origen could not effectively alter the text'.[20] There were many Old Latin (OL) versions in circulation, and Jerome's task, given to an unwilling writer by Pope Damasus in 382, was to produce a standard text. Jerome went 'to the very fountains themselves', as King James's translators stated, performing his work with 'great learning , judgment, industry , and faithfulness'.[21]

The history of the Vulgate is complex and what we have today is a revision of Jerome's work. Evangelicals could go out and give a good Bible study using the *Vulgate*, provided they found Latin readers! If the intention of the Pope was to pervert the Christian faith as Protestants understand it, he missed a great opportunity.

Papal supremacy?

Wilkinson's claim that Jerome's translation supports 'such doctrines as the papal supremacy, purgatory, celibacy of the priesthood, vigils, worship of relics, and the burning of daylight candles' could only have been made by someone who had never looked at it.[22] Critics of Jerome could have pointed out that 'do penance' (*poenitentiam agite*), is a very different concept from 'repent', 'turn around' (*metanoeite*), and appears to undermine the traditional system of penance (Matt. 3:1, 2; 4:17).

As regards clerical celibacy, the Vulgate accurately, translates (*unius uxor vir*) an undisputed Greek text which may be translated 'the husband of one wife' or 'married only once.' (1 Tim. 3:2; Titus 1:6). The Latin may be equally validly understood either way, although Jerome himself was a strong advocate of celibacy, and knew how he understood the words. The Jerusalem Bible (Catholic) adopts the second option, as does the 1981 Swedish version (ecumenical). The Catholic Challoner translation, a revision of the Douai, says 'husband of one wife', and supplies a footnote. In most communions any distinctive teaching is given in explanatory notes rather than manipulating the text.

Corrupted codices?

If the Vaticanus and Sinaiticus have been tampered with by Roman Catholics, we may ask why Catholic teachings are not introduced. Hell, the immortal soul, purgatory, transubstantiation (apparently Matthew 26:26 'this is my body' was enough), the role of Peter, Mary, the saints, good works, auricular confession are no more prominent in the so-called Catholic manuscripts than in the Textus Receptus, the manuscripts underlying the AV New Testament. Conspiracy? The charge is plausible only to those who are obsessed with conspiracy theory, and shut their eyes to facts. Now the New Age can be added to this list of villains as we shall see.[23]

Gail Anne Riplinger

G. A. Riplinger, *New Age Bible Versions*, represents a great deal of reading both from New Age sources, though often through anti-cult writers, and superficial New Testament scholarship. Unfortunately, the 690 pages are difficult reading for those who look for a balanced assessment of evidence. The New Age plotters and perverters runs, it appears, from Philo (died c. AD 42, after the OT was translated into Greek, and before the first of the NT books were composed), the heretic Marcion (c. 80–c. 160), who prepared an abbreviated canon of NT books, admitting only an edited Luke out of the four gospels, the allegorizing church father Origen, down to Philip Schaff, B. F. Westcott and F. J. A. Hort, J. B. Phillips and later scholars. The Roman Catholic Church does not escape either.

Riplinger appeals to 'conspiracy buffs'.[24] The arguments are irrefutable by definition since she can label all who differ with her as conspirators. The Bible clearly indicates that there is a 'great controversy' between God and Satan, between good and evil. This is no cause for a spiritual paranoia, and the delight of believing that one possesses some secret knowledge. It would not be worth mentioning such an incredible book were it not that it fits in with and feeds the apocalyptic, conspiracy phobias afflicting some groups in modern Western society.

Riplinger's loose way of working is quickly shown in the statement that at least 'five new version editors have permanently lost their ability to speak', another became insane, the editor of 'the reference dictionary used . . . to research Greek etymology was edited by Hitler's propaganda high priest, who was later . . . found guilty of war crimes'.[25] This is a reference to Gerhard Kittel (1888-1948), the editor, not the author of the whole massive *Theological Dictionary of the New Testament*, translated by the rather conservative Geoffrey W. Bromiley, and published by Eerdmans, not known for sponsoring liberal views.

Riplinger is correct in pointing out that unintelligent use of a lexicon or theological dictionary will not lead to sound exegesis.[26] She does, however, quote from Kittel's *TDNT* when it supports her argument. She falls into the very error she condemns when she links the words 'In the *process* of time' (Gen. 4:3, 5, version unspecified) with Process Theology.[27] This is on the level of arguing back from dynamite to *dunamis* (power). Alfred Nobel was not thinking theologically when he named his new explosive. (Of course, dynamo, producer of electrical power, comes from the same root.)

The conspiracy surfaces, 'The few Greek manuscripts underlying the new versions contain yet unreleased material which is an exact blueprint for the antichrist's One World Religion'.[28] How is it that with facsimiles of both Sinaiaticus (Aleph) and Vaticanus (B) available to all who can read them, this 'unreleased material' remains a secret known only to Riplinger and her allies.

Riplinger condemns the corrupt LXX readings slipped into the Bible to create a new Vulgate. She does not explain how it is that in the TR many of the OT quotations, even some ascribed to Jesus, are from the LXX reading. The argument is that the LXX, as we have it today, is the product of Origen.[29]

Marginal comments

There are certainly marginal comments in the Vaticanus. Jan Marcussen raises the alarm over the fact that there are later annotations, 'corrections' and alterations in the MSS he abhors.[30] Manuscripts were often 'mass-produced' by several writers taking dictation. Monks copying from one manuscript to another could skip a passage, or sometimes incorporate into the text the marginal notes of a previous copyist. Finished manuscripts were examined by a corrector, and his emendations are in a different hand. The fact that the emendations are visible means that readers were able to judge for themselves the likely authenticity of the text. The use of infra-red or ultra-violet light may make it easier to detect faint text, especially in the case of a palimpsest, a parchment from which the original writing has been erased, and new writing superimposed, but there is nothing sinister in this.[31] At Hebrews 1:3 a scribe restored a reading which a corrector had altered, scribbling, 'Fool and knave, can't you leave the old reading alone and not alter it?'[32]

Some critics believe that both Aleph and B originated through the efforts of Eusebius (of Nicomedia, d. 341/2), and Jerome (c.345–c.419) building upon Origen to produce a Bible for Constantine (c. 274/288–347).[33] The theory is flimsy and assumes what it seeks to prove.

The issue of 'corruption' cuts both ways. Bart D. Ehrman argues for a corruption of Scripture, but in the direction of orthodoxy, so as to deal with the Adoptionists, who believed Jesus was 'adopted' as the Son of God at His baptism, and Docetists, who believed that Jesus only appeared to be human. Such changes from the autographs, Ehrman affirms, were not towards heresy, but a clarification and support of orthodox theology.[34]

How should such intolerance be understood: 'The zeal

of thine house hath eaten me up', or 'they have a zeal of
God, but not according to knowledge' (John 2:17; Rom.
10:2)?

The selective quotation, the unverifiable slur, the
fantasy, give an unpromising start to what purports to be
a scholarly study of Bible versions, although Riplinger
seeks to document her assertions later in the text.

SOME SPECIFIC ISSUES

Charity or Love?

Some critics worry over the use in modern translations
of 'love' in place of 'charity', as a translation of *agape*.
They rightly note that love is used with a variety of meanings, while *agape* was distinguished from sensual love and
friendship love.[35] However, charity itself has changed its
meaning. (Tyndale used 'love' in 1 Corinthians 13). The
AV itself is not consistent in translating *agape*, using love
seventy-two times compared with twenty-seven uses of
charity. There seems no clear contextual reason for the
choice of one word over the other. Again we are
reminded of the AV translators' statement that they did
not feel bound to use only one English word to corres-
pond to a word in the original language. Charity has no
verb form in English, so the verb *agapao* had to be translated as love, unless some newly-coined English word
were supplied.

You in prayer

Is it right to use 'you' in addressing the Lord? It is true
that the Hebrew and Greek use the second person
singular, 'thee, thou'. In the language of 1611, thee and
thou were used for addressing family, intimates, inferiors,
and by a recognition of the Fatherhood of God, in prayer.
The respectful form of address was 'you'. The early
Quakers were in trouble with the law because they

refused to use 'you', which they saw as 'man-worship'. By Jesus' and Paul's use of 'Abba' we learn that God is to be addressed in the way that a child would speak to a parent. The Greek NT is written in the speech of the time, not some elevated liturgical language. The ordinary language receives its grace, beauty and power from the content, not the form. Reverence is more than a matter of archaic word forms. The tension is to preserve a necessary reverence in addressing the Lord, while not having to resort to a special language that is remote from daily living, and virtually unintelligible to the uninitiated. On the other hand, the loss of the second person singular in modern translations means that we lose the distinction Jesus drew in 'Simon, Simon, behold, Satan hath desired to have you (plural, all the disciples), that he may sift you (plural) as wheat: But I have prayed for thee (Peter), that thy faith fail not' (Luke 22:31, 32).

Nazarene

Riplinger states the term 'Nazarene' is used only in a derogatory way (Acts 24:5) and that new versions call Jesus 'the Nazarene' a dozen times, of which she cites three examples, all of which the NIV translates as 'Jesus of Nazareth'.[36] Riplinger is correct that Acts 24:5 implies a sneer at the Christians. In fact, Christians accepted the name and made it honourable. Quaker and Methodist were both names bestowed by their enemies. The word translated 'Nazarene' (*Nazoraios*) is that used by Matthew (2:23). Was the evangelist prophesying that the term Nazarene would be a term of contempt? (Acts 4:10; 6:14; John 19:19.) In fact, the more usual term is *Nazarenos*, not Matthew's less common word. Luke uses both words apparently interchangeably, showing that there is no difference in meaning. Since the angel actually used the words 'Jesus the Nazarene' (*Iesouv ton Nazarenon*) referring to the risen Lord (Mark 16:6), it is hard to see the point of Riplinger's argument. Nazarene may be used by New Agers; it is also the name of a highly respected Protestant denomination.

Exegesis and textual criticism

Sometimes exegesis and textual criticism (criticism meaning here a choice between variants) go hand in hand. In John 1:34, did John the Baptist say 'Son of God' (AV, RSV, NIV) or 'Chosen One' (NEB, JB)? The manuscript evidence is divided. Fee argues that 'Chosen One' is probably the original, echoing Psalm 2:7 or Isaiah 42:1.[37] We need fear neither adoptionism in the choice of Son, nor some diminishing of deity in the words Chosen One.

Riplinger sees a New Age plot to substitute 'the One' for other readings.[38] There is little consistency in her case, except the conspiracy theory which dictates that whenever any versions differs from the AV there must be evil motives. The capitalization in the NASB of the word 'one' in the AV reading is seen as New Age propaganda.[39] The word 'God' does not appear in the TR in the examples cited, and the NIV correctly reflects this.

To condemn the Five Points of Calvinism as a Satanic pentagram is a gross and unjustified attack on a respected wing of Christian thought.[40]

Detailed criticism

Some criticisms of modern translations seem so trivial that it is hard to see what is gained or lost. For example, did the soldiers offer Jesus vinegar which means here cheap sour wine (*oxos*) AV, or wine (*oinos*) NIV (Matt. 27:34)? Mark uses *oinos* for the same incident, suggesting that the issue is not crucial. Dean Burgon felt the textual evidence for vinegar was highly convincing, though Fee appears to have effectively demolished this.[41] Mark 15:36

indicates and Luke 23:36 implies from its position in the narrative that there was a second drink offered to Jesus, and they agree that this was sour wine, the cheap drink of the soldier. I am not sure what theological issue there is between wine and vinegar. Jesus tasted, but did not drink it, for He would accept nothing to deaden the pain He bore for us.

Riplinger compares the AV translation 'servant' with the NIV 'slave' for the Greek word *doulos*, as if there were something sinister in the latter usage.[42] This flies in the face of the original, for any Bible lexicon or word book will show that the *doulos* was a bondservant, not a free person. The glory of the Gospel is that the former slaves of sin become slaves of Jesus Christ (Rom. 6:17, 18), bought with a price (1 Cor. 6:20), yet standing free in liberty (Gal. 5:1).

The divine name

The substitution of 'the Lord' for the name Jehovah alarms Riplinger and others. There are religious groups who prominently insist on using the holy name. Hebrew has no vowels as such, and the divine name, known to us as Jehovah, was written with four consonants, the tetragrammaton. This sacred name Yahweh, is sometimes translated as Jehovah in the AV, but predominantly as LORD, in capitals to distinguish it from Adonai, Lord, as for example in Psalm 110:1. Barker discusses the problems faced by the translator of *YHWH*, both when Yahweh stands alone, and when combined with Sabaoth (armies, or hosts, hence LORD of hosts, AV). The very holiness of the name Yahweh led to the substitution of Adonai in reading aloud. The Greek *kurios* was used in the LXX as a translation of Adonai, and used in place of Yahweh where the priests said Adonai.[43] If the substitution of LORD for Jehovah is wrong in the new versions, we may question how Riplinger overlooks it in the AV. She does not quote the Catholic Jerusalem Bible which almost uniformly uses Yahweh.[44]

Riplinger cites Calvin Linton of the NIV Committee, who stated that the translator's theological bias 'may colour the text or even misrepresent it'.[45] Martin Luther introduced the word 'alone', which Paul did not write, into his German translation to emphasize his point (Rom. 3:28). Are we then to suppose that the scholars of 1611 themselves came with no theological baggage?

Word for word

Riplinger seems to fall victim to the exegetical fallacy that an English word will necessarily carry the precise meaning of the word in the original tongue. 'Hell' is an example of a word used to translate *she'ol* (Hebrew) and *Hades* (Greek). The question for the translators is whether the Bible writer had in mind the eternally burning hell of many Christian believers. The Hebrew *she'ol* has a wide range of meanings.[46] The Catholic Jerusalem Bible, which might be expected to promote the idea of hell, reads *she'ol* in the messianic Psalm 16:10. Riplinger feels that heresy is taught if the translator transliterates rather than translates the original terms used for the resting place (place of torment?) of the dead. New Agers would appear to be counter-working orthodox Catholicism if the doctrine of hell is removed. Christian belief is too firmly based to be dependent on the way a particular noun is translated.

Lucifer

Riplinger is concerned that the omission of the word 'Lucifer' from Isaiah 14:12 breaks the connection, noted by Tertullian, between the ambitious pretender of Isaiah's prophecy and Satan. She is correct in that many expositors, incorrectly in my view, do not see a cosmic reference in the passage, but incorrect in her reasoning on the underlying Hebrew word *helel*. Strong's concordance gives 'morning star' as the rendering of this term which occurs only once in the OT. Riplinger is concerned that the title 'morning star' applied to the Lord Jesus (Rev. 22:16) is also given to the usurper of Isaiah 14:12.[47] The word Lucifer is taken from the Vulgate, and does not appear as such in the Hebrew. Luther used 'schoener Morgenstern', beautiful morning star. Perhaps Riplinger has not seen the full arrogance of the boaster who claims a title of divinity that will be used by the Son of God.

Teacher or master?

Riplinger cites twenty-five examples where the AV 'master' is translated in the NIV and NSB by 'teacher' (*didaskolos*), and four by 'rabbi', a transliteration of the Aramaic via Greek.[48] It seems hard to blame translators for using the terms of the original language, especially as the AV itself uses 'rabbi' of Jesus in four instances, and of John the Baptist in one. The intensive form 'rabboni' is found in two places (Mark 10:51; John 20:16). (The AV has 'teacher' as a marginal reading for 'master' in Mary's cry.) Riplinger sees 'teacher' as a word acceptable to the New Age. However, she has overlooked the fact the 'master' is also a term hi-jacked (a term she might approve of!) by the New Age.

Do new versions teach asceticism or not? If the omission of fasting from Mark 9:29 is a move to weaken good Christian practice, then one must ask why Catholicising trends would diminish ascetic ideas rather than stress fasting. Perhaps, in this instance New Age has prevailed.[49] On the other hand, Riplinger objects to the translation of 1 Corinthians 9:27 ('keep under my body' in the AV) as 'beat, or bruise', seeing here pagan practices of flagellation from Delphi to birch twigs in a sauna.[50] The Greek word seems to derive from the world of boxing, literally to give a black eye, treat roughly. Of course, if one regards lexicons and dictionaries as tainted, then one can translate as one wishes.

Other writers claim that new discoveries of 'Gnostic' gospels show that the NT account of Christianity is incorrect. The conspiracy theory is invoked to argue that the Church suppressed its Gnostic rivals, who may have been the true heirs of Jesus. Theories come, make a splash, and then peter out.

The angry Fundamentalist conspiratorial theories often serve more to arouse suspicion of other's motives than to bring comfort and assurance from the Word of God. By wildly over-stating their case, the conspiracy buffs may make a conservative approach appear ridiculous. Evangelicalism is not guilty by association with the wilder extremists, but sometimes the reading public may be confused.

This has been a painful chapter to write, for there is so much evil abroad, there is a strong New Age movement. Not everything that Riplinger wrote is nonsense, but the medium is the message, and the valuable fragments are drowned in shrillness. 'Unclean spirits' are active. The dragon, the beast and the false prophet, an unholy trinity of evil, were foreshadowed, but so was their final destruction (Rev. 16:13; 20:10). What a pity that the defenders of the Fundamentals sometimes shout so raucously, so hysterically, and mingle sense with nonsense that their cause is damaged. The Authorized Version does have sober defenders. No one should be disturbed in their devotion to the 1611 text. Its worth is undeniable. It deserves good friends, not those whose style spoils the substance.

'Nevertheless, the foundation of God standeth sure.'
(2 Tim. 2:19.)
'Nevertheless, God's solid foundation stands firm.'
(2 Tim. 2:19, NIV.)

---

[1]Verrecchia, pages 15, 16.
[2]Duthie, page 211.
[3]London: John Murray, 1883.
[4]Burgon, page 29.
[5]Burgon, page 11.
[6]Burgon, pages 35-40.
[7]Burgon, page 77.
[8]'Problem Passages of the New Testament in Some Modern Translations', The Expository Times, 87 (1975-76), 214, 215; Carson, Debate, pages 63-65.
[9]Beegle, pages 95-97; Vine, 1975, DNTT, 2:723-725.
[10]Riplinger, page 83; cf. R. L. Longenecker in Barker The making of a contemporary translation, pages 164-175.
[11]Barker, page 173.
[12]Burgon, page 99.
[13]Wilbur N. Pickering, The Identity of the New Testament Text, Nashville, TN: Thomas Nelson, 1977.
[14]'A Critique of W. N. Pickering's The Identity of the New Testament Text. A Review Article' Westminster Theological Journal, 41 (1978) 397-423; D. A. Carson Debate 15. Carson, Debate, pages 43-78.
[15]Pickering, page 140.
[16]Debate, page 36, emphasis supplied.
[17]Wilkinson, page 186.
[18]Wilkinson, pages 45, 46.
[19]Pickering, pages 108, 109.
[20]Opfell, page 149.
[21]Wilkinson, page 45.
[22]Duthie, pages 213-216 for other examples of ill-informed criticism.
[23]Riplinger, page 420.
[24]Riplinger, page 593.
[25]D. A. Carson, Exegetical Fallacies, Grand Rapids, MI: Baker Book House, 1984, pages 25-66.
[26]Riplinger, pages 247, 288, 333.
[27]Riplinger, page 3.
[28]Riplinger, pages 139, 536, 537.
[29]Jan Marcussen, '20 Theses . . . '.
[30]Metzger, 1964, pages 8-35.
[31]Metzger 1964, page 196.
[32]Riplinger, page 534.
[33]Bart D. Ehrman, The Orthodox Corruption of Scripture: The Effects of

Early Christological Controversies on the Text of the New Testament, New York, Oxford: Oxford University Press, 1993.

[34]Riplinger, page 602, rightly notes that the two Greek words *phileo* and *agapao* used for 'love' must be judged by context rather than each having clearly differentiated meanings.

[35]Riplinger pages 368, 369. Matthew's use of Nazoraios may be a play on the word *neser* (branch) in Isaiah 11:1, or, less likely *nasir*, one who took the Nazirite vow (Numbers 6:1, 2).

[36]Epp and Fee, page 16.

[37]Riplinger, pages 76-97.

[38]Riplinger, page 87.

[39]Riplinger, page 231.

[40]Fee 1978, pages 417, 418.

[41]Riplinger, pages 233-235.

[42]Barker, pages 143-150.

[43]Riplinger, pages 372-378.

[44]Riplinger, page 394.

[45]TWOT 2:892, 893.

[46]Riplinger, pages 39-55.

[47]Riplinger, pages 322-329.

[48]Riplinger, page 71.

[49]Riplinger, pages 127-129.

CHAPTER NINE

A cloud of witnesses
Hebrews 12:1

Manuscripts as witnesses

The word 'witness' is often used in textual notes as a reference to Bible manuscripts, as, for example, in the New International Version. This is similar, though more precise, than the marginal readings of the AV. There is indeed a cloud of NT witnesses, around 5,000, but their very profusion, and the number and variety of translations into English may leave some readers in a fog, rather than a cloud. Can it be the Word of God if it doesn't read exactly the same? That question was looked at earlier, realizing that the history of translation goes back to New Testament times. In the previous chapter types of translation were considered. Now you have come into a bookshop to buy a Bible. But which one? One is actually called Holy Bible, another is just Bible, and there are other names. What should you choose?

If you are looking for the old tradition, remember that the AV itself was modified, so that the text today is not quite the same as that of 1611. This is either forgotten or unknown to those who argue strongly for the exact wording of the AV. They have probably never seen a 1611 edition, which incidentally included the Apocrypha or Deuterocanonical (Second canon) books.

The Revised Version

The first notable break with the English tradition was the *Revised Version* of 1881-85, fifteen years after the Convocation of Canterbury voted for the plan. The New Testament, relying heavily on the textual work of

Westcott and Hort, aroused some fierce criticism, as noted earlier, although the changes were not sufficiently significant to attract the attention of the average reader. The RV never gained much popularity, and today it is virtually unused. Anglicans had 1611 language in the Bible readings in the 1662 Prayer Book, although the Psalter uses the Great Bible of 1540. The *American Standard Version* of 1901, itself a revision of the Revised Version of 1881-85, updating the RV and eliminating Briticisms, was hindered in acceptance by its use of Jehovah throughout in place of the AV 'the LORD', 'disastrous from the point of the liturgical, homiletical and devotional use of the Bible. The other factor was the preservation of the word order of the original, which made for awkward English'.[1]

A pioneer quartet

Four modern speech versions were important in their day. *The Twentieth Century New Testament* (1904) was a response to two letters from parents complaining that their children could not understand the language of the AV or RV. The definitive edition was published both in London and New York. One of the most remarkable features of this corporate work was the age range (19-63), and the occupational and religious range of the translators: ministers, housewives, businessmen and teachers from at least five denominations. The Moody Press reprinted this version, with some modifications in 1961. It is still a very good and readable version.

Richard Francis Weymouth (1822-1902), a notable classical scholar, was headmaster at Mill Hill School, near London, and on his retirement commenced *The New Testament in Modern Speech: an idiomatic translation into everyday English* (1909), a project he did not live to complete. He hoped his version would be a supplement to, not a replacement for, the main versions. The fourth Weymouth edition appeared in 1929. It reads well even today, and because of the editorial work done upon it does not suffer from the idiosyncrasies of some one-person translations.

James Moffatt (1870-1944) 'endeavoured to translate the New Testament exactly as one would render any piece of contemporary Hellenistic prose, hoping to convey to the reader something of the direct homely impression made by the original upon those for whom it was written'.[2] *The New Testament* was first published in 1913. This complete break with earlier translations suffered from an overuse of textual conjectures and rearrangements without firm manuscript support. For example, John 15 and 16 'are restored to their original position in the middle of (13) verse 31'. He failed to convince most scholars of the correctness of this transplant surgery, which relies in Moffatt's conjecture on how the text should read, rather than manuscript evidence. His Old Testament (1924) was more startling. Regarding the OT text as 'often desperately corrupt', he emended (corrected as he thought fit), conjectured and transposed very freely.

> 'Do not rest content with curiously noting the differences between this version of the Bible and its predecessors, especially the Authorized English Version, but try to understand and to appreciate their common aim. The object of any translation ought to resemble the object of its original, and in this case it is not mere curiosity, not even intellectual interest.'[3]

Moffatt's work raises the question of how much authority the translator has over the text. While it is necessary to find the best reading possible, the process goes too far when wholesale changes are made, however impressive the conjectures. Moffatt illustrates both the freedom and brilliance, but also the dangers of a one-person version.

Edgar Johnson Goodspeed (1871-1962), a prolific American scholar in New Testament studies, accepted the challenge to produce a translation of his own. He aimed at a readable version, free of Briticisms, both for private and public use. It was tested on congregations as he proceeded. The NT appeared in 1923, and the complete *Holy Bible. An American Translation* in 1931. Although little used today, these four versions helped to break the mould of Bible translation, and prepared the way for the Revised Standard Version.

The call for new translations

A vote in 1937 by the International Council on Religious Education resulted in the *Revised Standard Version of the New Testament* (1946), and complete Bible in 1952. The Greek text underlying the NT was eclectic, drawing from a range of sources and not tied to any of the standard editions. The OT was based mainly, but not exclusively on the Masoretic text. As its name implies, the RSV is a revision of earlier version, and strong echoes of the AV, the RV and the American Standard Version. Foster considers the RSV liberal, making prophecy inharmonious with fulfilment (for example, Isa. 7:14; Matt. 1:23), and weakening the testimony to the deity of Christ.[4] The second point arises from the fact that the RSV translators used the old singular forms *thee* and *thou* when addressing Deity. How then should the disciples address Jesus in the gospels? 'We know that Jesus was God; did the disciples?', replied one of the RSV translators. Foster notes other instances where he feels belief has distorted the translation. He seems to define 'liberal' as disbelief in verbal inspiration.[5]

Tyndale can be heard via the language of the AV taken into the RSV. In this sense it is conservative in its approach, but was attacked quite fiercely by some fundamentalists.[6] Some were so incensed, particularly in the United States, that copies of the RSV were publicly burned, an action that says more about the protesters than the literary or spiritual value of the translation. The divine name was printed as LORD, reverting to the AV practice. A Roman Catholic version of the *RSV New Testament* appeared in 1956, and the complete Bible with Apocrypha in 1966. The Catholic edition is closer to the Received Text than the RSV, including the long ending of Mark (16:9-20), a paradox for those who have seen anti-Protestant tendencies in deviations from the TR.

A changing world

The increasing social informality of the 1960s and early 70s, both in the secular and religious world, typified in Roman Catholicism by the Mass in current English, and the Anglican Alternative Service Book, led to a further look at the Bible in English. Another factor was the pressure to remove 'sexist' language. The third aim was to incorporate the results of sound biblical scholarship. The committee that worked on the *New Revised Standard Version* (1989) included Roman Catholic scholars, which had not been the case for the RSV. *The Common Bible* edition of the RSV with Apocrypha (1973) is acceptable to Roman Catholics, Greek Orthodox and Protestants. Consensus on a translation does not mean that any party compromised its beliefs. The Common Bible meant that for the first time each group could discuss teachings from an agreed biblical platform. Many scholars regard the RSV and the NRSV as among the best study Bibles.

The Modern Language Bible (MLB) or *New Berkeley Version in Modern English* (1945, 1959, 1969 (revised edition)) was initiated by the Dutch-American Gerrit Verkuyl, a Presbyterian, and his work is especially evident in the NT. Published by Zondervan, 'the MLB is a monument to evangelical scholarship . . . a useful tool to compare with other versions . . . '.[7]

The New English Bible (NEB, 1970) was a British inter-denominational enterprise, with Roman Catholic observers. The New Testament appeared in 1961 and the complete Bible in 1970. In four years 6,000,000 copies of the New Testament were sold, although, as D. E. Nineham remarked: 'No one of course knows how many of these copies have been read.'[8] The NEB was the first completely new committee translation.

Instead of the formal, word-for-word translation principle of the RSV, the NEB sought to understand the original as precisely as possible, 'and then saying again in our own native idiom what we believed the author to be saying in his': in other words, dynamic equivalence.[9] The translators had three classes of readers in mind. ' . . . first . . . the large proportion of the population with which the Church had no communication, and which found traditional versions unintelligible. The second was the younger generation, and the third the "intelligent people who do attend church", but for whom the traditional language of the Bible had lost its impact through too great familiarity'.[10]

Reviews of the NEB New Testament focused, in their various ways, on four issues. First, the quality of the Greek text employed. The translators did not tie themselves to any of the printed Greek texts, but felt free to select readings they felt were the best. Kubo and Specht noted the rather curious choice of some weakly attested NT readings.

Secondly, the accuracy of the translation and the quality of the critical apparatus (notes on textual variations) provided both for the Greek and non-Greek reader.

The third, and most imponderable area, was the question of style. 'Timeless English' is hard to achieve. Some reviewers felt that the language was a worthy successor to the AV. Others criticised its use of unidiomatic or scholarly words. Was the translation ever tested on the pews? What is gained, for example, by altering the AV 'ministering spirits' to 'ministrant spirits' in Hebrews 1:14?[11] In other parts, some reviewers felt that the NEB descended into the 'crudely colloquial, awkward, indiscreet and inappropriate'.[12] Transatlantic reviewers pointed out that the translation contained a number of Briticisms an American readership found hard to understand. The level of translation was felt by most reviewers to be high, though with some inconsistencies. Any translator faces the problem of whether to be consistent in rendering a Greek word into one given English word. To stay woodenly with word-to-word correspondence may lose nuances of the Greek. To introduce variations may miss the writer's intention that the resonances of a word should echo through the passage. The NEB may have overdone variation for variation's sake.

Questions about doctrines

The fourth, and most critical issue, is theological. Is the translation true to the theology of the New Testament? As the NEB was a British production, and did not make a great impact in the United States, it was spared the public burnings of the RSV.

A number of doctrinal issues were raised by reviewers. First, is there any significance in substituting 'God's justice' for the 'righteousness of God' in Romans 3:5.[13] T. H. Brown states, 'Countless alterations betray the dogmatic bias of the translators against the reformed faith of our fathers.' The changes include, at least to Brown, casting doubt on the Virgin Birth and the supplying of the indefinite article which does not exist in Greek. The use of 'Thee' and 'Thou' is inconsistent and appears to give less honour to the Son than to the Father. The omission of 'God' from 1 Timothy 3:16 is noted. Concessions to Rome are seen in Matthew 16:18 and Acts 13:2, together with Luke 3:21; Acts 3:11, and Romans 15:16. The atonement appears to be weakened (1 John 2:2; Col. 1:4). Imputed Righteousness, and the Effectual Calling are weakened towards a Pelagian, self-help religion. The rendering of 2 Timothy 3:16 implies the partial rather than the plenary inspiration of Scripture. As for language, Brown found it more difficult than the AV, pedantic, not contemporary, crude, and in places unseemly, where modern English brings out things best left in decent obscurity of the AV.[14] H. P. Hamann, a Lutheran, felt that Justification by Faith seems 'strangely weaker' in the NEB.[15] The translators might ask both Brown and Hamann how far their doctrine depends on a particular translation. In turn, Brown and Hamann might ask how far doctrine has influenced the NEB translators. *The Revised English Bible* was published in 1989, and has eliminated some of the problems associated with the earlier NEB.

The Good News Bible, Today's English Version (GNB, TEV, 1976). The complete GNB, a project initiated by the American Bible Society, incorporated the fourth edition of the New Testament. This is a dynamic equivalence translation in easily understood English, spoken rather than written, colloquial rather than literary, but avoiding slang. For the sake of clarity, modern idioms sometimes replace those of the original. (We may remind ourselves that even the AV occasionally expanded or changed a figure of speech, as in Judges 9:29, where the word God is not in the Hebrew.) Technical terms such as centurion are changed to modern parallels, and technical religious language is modernized wherever possible. The notes are valuable and not intrusive. The GNB is valuable for personal and for public worship, but those who want to study closely will wish to compare it with a translation such as the NRSV.

The New King James Version (NKJV, 1982). Objections to the AV/KJV focus largely on the difficulty of the language and the textual basis. There may be some who would insist on the verbal inspiration of the AV. There are certainly those who call it 'inspired', without defining the term. As was mentioned earlier, the AV has been revised several times. The NKJV project began in 1975 with a group of conservative Bible scholars in America. 'All participating scholars have signed a document of subscription to the plenary and verbal inspiration of the original autographs of the Bible.'

The NKJV translators claim that the NKJV 'follows the historic precedent of the Authorized Version in maintaining a literal approach to translation, except where the idiom of the original language cannot be translated directly into our tongue'.[16] The NKJV dropped the second person singular, thee, thou, thy and thine. This involved the verb forms also, doing away with the 'sayest' and 'doest' and the obsolete 'saith' and 'doeth' that intimidated many a youthful reader. Other verb forms were modernized, for example, 'show' for 'shew'. Obsolete or outmoded words have been replaced, and the modern understanding of both biblical Greek and Hebrew have been employed to translate the originals more accurately. A number of idiomatic phrases have been updated.

The NKJV uses the Traditional or Majority Greek text. It is the only important modern translation not to be

based on a modern critical text, but there are notes referring to other possible readings, omissions or insertions.
Those who feel at home with the AV, but would like a
more up-to-date version, removing some obscurities of
1611, should welcome the NKJV, which should give them
the benefits of both ancient and modern.

The *21st Century King James Version* is less well known
than the NKJV. It claims to be 'an accurate and understandable upgrading' of the KJV, while 'retaining the
power, beauty and timeless message which has been
saving souls for 400 years'. If we are to believe the 'blurb',
it is 'closer in language and spirit to the King James
Version than any other Bible. It is simply the most power-
fully worded of all modern Bibles'.[17] Whether or not this
is true, Christians have certainly learned marketing hype.
The fact that it is not published by one of the major
companies may be a reason for its lack of popularity.

The *New Geneva Study Bible* is an update of the
Geneva Bible of 1560, by a team headed by the
distinguished evangelical, J. I. Packer. It is the 'first study
Bible in the Reformed (Calvinist) tradition'.

The *New International Version* (NIV, 1978) is the most
widely used of the modern translations into English.
Though modern, it is quite conservative, upholding the
'traditional' reading or something close to it in both of
the above cases.

The translators were an international, multi-
denominational Protestant group, reflecting a desire to
reach a wide English readership. So the work is
transdenominational and transnational. This translation
has had a far greater impact on the English-speaking
world than the NEB, although the NEB seems to have
influenced the NIV.

'The translators were united in their commitment to
the authority and infallibility of the Bible as God's Word

in written form.' Their 'first concern (was) the accuracy of the translation and fidelity to the thought of the biblical writers'. They sought 'clear and natural English . . . idiomatic but not idiosyncratic', reflecting the differing styles of the biblical authors. The translators 'sought to preserve some measure of continuity with the long tradition of translating the Scriptures into English'.[18] The result is 'a middle of the road version in which a high degree of formal correspondence is combined with renderings that are dynamically equivalent'.[19] As far as possible, the traditional familiar religious terminology is retained, though words such as 'peculiar' are changed to reflect the meaning of the original.

Stephen W. Paine, one of the translators of the NIV, stated that it was required of all NIV translators that they 'believe in the inerrancy of Scripture'. Paine illustrates this by showing that Matthew's citation of Isaiah 7:14 will determine the translation of *almah* as 'young woman' or 'virgin'.[20]

The Masoretic Text was the basis of the Old Testament, with some use of the Dead Sea scrolls and the ancient versions, the Septuagint and the Vulgate. The Greek NT text was an eclectic one, using the 'best current printed texts'.[21]

It is interesting to note that the 1973 edition of the NT was revised in the direction of more traditional wording in 1978. The text is set out in paragraphs with inconspicuous verse numbers that do not intrude into the readability. The paragraph headings are useful. A parallel is the chapter summaries in many printings of the AV. There are nearly 3,350 footnotes, giving alternative readings, alternative translations, or explanations. Traditionalists who may be shocked by this should look again in the marginal readings and italicised words of the AV.

The Making of a Contemporary Translation, contains

fifteen essays, explaining different aspects of the translators' work and methods.[22] Some of the essays deal with
matters of policy: 'The importance of literary style in
Bible translation today'; 'The footnoting system'; 'When
the Spirit was poetic', the best way to render Hebrew
poetry into English. 'When literal is not accurate,' deals
with the need to translate thought and meaning rather
than word for word. A lesser linguistic London fog was
avoided by 'Anglicizing the NIV'.

When a NT writer has quoted from the OT, the translator has to decide how far the NT should influence the
translation of the Old. The translator's view of inspiration
will guide the decision. This issue arises in 'Old Testament Quotations in the New Testament,' and in the case
study, 'Translation problems in Psalms 2 and 4'.

Earl Kalland indicates 'How the Hebrew and Aramaic
Old Testament text was established', Larry Walker
explains 'How the NIV made use of new light on the
Hebrew text'. More controversial issues are Ralph Earle's
'The rationale for an eclectic text'; 'Why the Hebrew
"She'ol" was translated "grave" '; the editor's 'YHWH
SABAOTH: The Lord Almighty', and Richard L.
Longenecker, 'The One and Only Son'. Edwin Palmer
rounded off the essays by asking, 'Isn't the King James
Version good enough?' (The KJV and the NIV compared.)

No translation is perfect

Of course, critics, can point to imperfections in the
NIV. The translators did not claim infallibility, and their
work is subject to revision. Occasionally their theological
interpretation shows through, as in the translation of
'Most Holy Place' in Hebrews 9:8, 12 where the Greek has
'the holies' (*ta hagia*). The Greek expression Holy of
Holies, or most holy place (*hagia hagion*) appears only in
Hebrews 9:3. A comparison of Mark 7:19 in the AV ('purg-

ing all meats') and the NIV ('in saying this he declared all foods clean') shows that the NIV has expanded the text that the AV left ambiguous, and perhaps obscure to the modern reader. Most modern translations agree with the NIV here.

Ed L. Miller has made a detailed study of the NIV translation of John's prologue, finding at least eleven important shortcomings in the eighteen verses. While not all the eleven are really important, 'some of these points involve astonishing "interpretational intrusions" beyond what is actually given in the text'.[23]

The New International Reader's Version (NIrV, 1996), is claimed to be 'even clearer and easier to understand than the NIV and scholars who produced it have made sure that they constantly referred back to the original Hebrew and Greek. So you don't have to worry about accuracy'. Dr David Hubbard states, 'Its simplicity, clarity and accuracy put God's Word within the reach of millions of persons who find standard translation beyond their grasp.'[24]

Key features of the NIrV are
* Accurate. By maintaining the familiar dignity for which the NIV is famous, new Bible readers can if they wish, move from the NIrV without difficulty.
* Readable. Shorter sentences retain the meaning of the original text but make the Scriptures more accessible . . . . Longer words are recast to enable readers with no previous Bible knowledge to grasp the meaning of the text more clearly.
* Clear. Ideal for both public and personal reading.
* Trustworthy. Top Christian leaders and Bible scholars recommend it.

'Blessed are the poor in spirit, for theirs is the kingdom of heaven.' (Matt. 5:3, NIV).

'Blessed are those who are spiritually needed.
The kingdom of heaven belongs to them.' (NIrV).[25]

The New American Standard Bible (NASB, 1971). The reason for this version was to perpetuate the qualities and values of the *American Standard Version* (1901), which was falling into disuse. The NASB project aimed 'to adhere to the original languages of the Holy Scriptures as closely as possible and at the same time obtain a fluent and readable style according to current English usage'.[26] The OT text used is a modern critical edition. Jehovah in the ASV is replaced by LORD. This also applies to place names, so what Abraham called 'Yahweh provides' (JB), Jehovah-jireh (ASV), becomes LORD Will Provide (Gen. 22:14, cf. Exod. 17:15). The NT text was the Nestle, 23rd edition, but strongly influenced by the Received Text. This makes the NASB more acceptable to conservatives, who might otherwise see some favourite passages altered or omitted. The single column format, with wide margins, and helpful notes and cross references are valuable features. Verses are set out as units, rather than clearly grouped in paragraphs. In defence of this, it may be argued that the originals had no paragraphs, and translators do not always agree where the breaks should occur. For instance does Paul start to talk about home and family at Ephesians 5:21 or 22? Starting at verse 21, 'Submit yourselves to one another . . . ' (NIV) is a healthy corrective to husbands who feel they have sort of freehold from verse 22, 'Wives, submit'. 'The morals of the home' begin at Ephesians 5:21 (JB), but 'Husbands and wives' at 5:22 (NIV).

The NASB is an excellent study Bible, although its determination to be faithful to the originals, including accurate rendering of the tenses of Greek verbs, has produced some unidiomatic English. The *Ryrie Study*

Bible is an up-date of the NASB, available only in the Ryrie edition. The 'thee' and 'thou' forms have been replaced. There are now 10,000 notes, 2,000 more than in the earlier Ryrie.

The *Everyday Bible* or The New Century Version (1988) has not achieved great popularity. Its use in the *Inspirational Bible* may broaden its appeal.

The *Contemporary English Version*, or Bible for Today's Family (1995) 'addresses the needs of those who read the Word publicly and those who hear it'. It assumes 'that the text should be easily understood by the hearer and the reader without aid of interpretation of language; that there should be a faithful communication from one language to another; and that the average reader can read the passage without stumbling'.[27]

The *God's Word Angel Bible* is advertised as 'the Bible that presents the full intended *meaning* (NB italics in print) of the original writers in crystal-clear contemporary English'.[28] This is a bold claim, particularly when a number of passages in Scripture are ambiguous, both ideas making sense and not ruling out the other, for example, John 5:39.

Roman Catholic versions

The Jerusalem Bible (JB, 1966) was the first complete modern Catholic Bible translation from the original languages (Ronald Knox's 1949 version stayed strictly with the 1592 edition of the Vulgate). The French Dominican *La Bible de Jerusalem* proved so popular that it was then translated into several other European languages. 'Most of the translation (into English) was made directly from the original languages. Some portions, however, were originally translated from the French, and the resulting translation was then compared with the Greek or Hebrew original.' The English version followed the text used by the French version and generally followed the interpretation found there. Was the JB a new translation? 'If JB is to be judged by the results rather than the procedures that were followed, it is a distinctly new and readable version.'[29]

The JB is considerably freer than the RSV, especially in the NT, but not as free as Phillips. The translators did not aim at paraphrase. The attitude to the originals is conservative, for example, Mark 16:9-20 is included without any indication that its textual basis is questioned. Conservative Protestants are likely to accept the note that the passage 'is included in the canonically accepted body of inspired scripture . . . this does not necessarily imply Marcan authorship . . . .' The notes are generally acceptable to Protestants, though a few give a Catholic interpretation. Naturally, where the original can, without distortion, be interpreted according to Catholic understanding, this has been done. The divine name is given as Yahweh rather than LORD or Jehovah.

The New Jerusalem Bible (NJB, 1985) followed a 1973 revision of the French *La Bible de Jerusalem*. The English revision was from the original languages rather than the French. The Standard Edition has extensive notes. Naturally these are Catholic in tone where there are controversial issues.

The New American Bible (NAB, 1970) project began in 1936 as a modern translation of the Vulgate. The 1943 papal encyclical *Divino Afflante Spiritu* of Pope Pius XII promoted biblical studies, and for the first time advocated that translators work from the original languages. Begun in 1944, the NAB may have suffered from the long time in preparation, so that the standard of translation is somewhat inconsistent. Although initiated by Roman

Catholic scholars, Protestant scholars were added after Vatican II, so the version is ecumenical.

The *Holy Bible: Standard Revised Catholic Version* is the latest revision of a long-standing text.

Paraphrases and expanded texts

The distinction between paraphrase and translation is not clear cut, and the versions mentioned below vary in the degree of freedom they take.

J. B. Phillips was prompted, like others before him, by the need to make the Bible intelligible to young people. The New Testament, completed in 1958, was issued in sections, starting with the Letters in 1947. The 1972/3 revision pruned out some of the excessive freedom and expansion of meaning found in 1958. Kubo and Specht write: 'The NT reads as if it were originally written in twentieth century English.'[30] At times it uses comparatively rare words, while in other places it is too colloquial. This again illustrates the disadvantages of a one-person translator. However, committee translations have not always avoided these problems. Phillips listened to his critics and the revised edition of 1972 is much more accurate.

J. B. Phillips vividly paraphrases Romans 12:2 to read, 'Don't let the world around you squeeze you into its own mould, but let God remould your mind from within.' The thought is clearly conveyed, but the vocabulary is not that of the original. A Bible word study cannot safely be based on a paraphrase.

The Living Bible: A Paraphrase (LB or LBP, 1971). Kenneth Taylor, an American businessman, though theologically trained, and deeply involved in Christian work, found that his own children did not understand the AV. As he sought to explain the meaning in modern plain English, he determined to produce a modern version.

Issued in parts, the complete *Living Bible* appeared in 1971. The LB is a translation of a translation as Taylor worked from the English text of the AV, rather than the original languages. The careful reader of Taylor's work will see that his interpretation has sometimes influenced the paraphrase beyond the boundaries of the original text, for example, Genesis 6:1-2, 4, though there is a qualifying footnote. In discussing the translator's role, Taylor stated, 'For when the Greek or Hebrew is not clear, then the theology of the translator is his guide along with his sense of logic.' He took 'a rigid evangelical position'.[31]

His theological stance comes out in his treatment of life after death, or the law.

'For Moses gave us only the Law with its rigid demands and merciless justice, while Jesus Christ brought us loving forgiveness as well.' (John 1:17.)

Notice how Taylor has added to the original. The Greek states that 'the law was given through Moses'. Both the Old Testament narrative, and the use of the passive, to indicate the action of God without using His name, make it clear that the law was not Moses' invention, as one might infer from Taylor.

The words 'with its rigid demands and merciless justice' are totally absent from the Greek. Taylor has subtracted from the original by substituting 'loving forgiveness' for grace and truth. 'Only' and 'as well' are not found in the Greek either actually or implied. In passing, we may note that 'but', implying a contrast between Moses and Jesus, is not in the Greek. John may have meant continuity, not a contrast. There are other examples of unwarranted expansion of the original: Matthew 22:32, Mark 12:27, Luke 20:38, Matthew 13:52. Without comparison with other versions, the reader is seldom able to separate the plain text from Taylor's expansion, a common problem with paraphrases. Good for devotional reading, and giving an easy-to-read overview, the LB is not a sound basis for doctrinal study.

The *New Living Translation* (NLT) is a scholarly and extensive revision of LB by ninety 'world-class scholars', intended as a 'general-purpose version'. For this reason it does not belong in a section on paraphrases.

'At last, the authority of the King James Version meets the warmth and clarity of The Living Bible.' The NLT may have tried to be too reader-friendly. For example, Jesus' 'hard saying' 'let the dead bury their own dead' (Matt. 8:22, NRSV) is sanitized to the rather bland (and interpretive), 'Let those who are spiritually dead care for their own dead.'[32]

The Amplified Bible (1975), published by Zondervan, followed earlier publication of John's gospel and the NT. 'Its purpose is to reveal, together with the single-word English equivalent to each key Hebrew and Greek word, any other clarifying shades of meaning that may be concealed by the traditional word-for-word method of translation. In this way, the reader will experience the width of meaning enjoyed by those who listened to or read the originals. In fact, the translation is 'a mini-commentary'. It can be useful, but it tends to overload the reader with information, giving multiple meanings for a word, sometimes without sufficient regard for the context. Though claiming to be 'free from private interpretation', theological bias appears in the amplification of Isaiah 7:14, 1 Peter 3:19, 20, and Matthew 16:18. There is a series of indicators to distinguish the basic translation from the amplifications, but in practice, without close attention, it is not easy to separate the two.

In preparing *The New Testament: A New Translation* (1968, 1969, 1980) William Barclay sought to 'make the New Testament intelligible to the man who is not a technical scholar', and 'to make a translation that does not need a commentary to explain it'.[33] Unfortunately, the translation itself becomes something of a commentary through its interpretation of some passages. The reader cannot, except by comparison with other versions, see where the Greek original ends and Barclay begins.

The Message (1993) a translation by Eugene Peterson, has sold in large numbers and received extravagant endorsements, so it has to be reckoned with. Unlike the LB *The Message* is not called a paraphrase, and the 'blurb' leads us to expect the work of a highly talented Greek scholar. There are many good things about Peterson's work, but it suffers from the common defect of a one-person version. There has been no committee of translators or readers to criticize and give a wider perspective. Verse numbers are omitted and this makes things difficult when verses are transposed as in 1 Corinthians 11:1-16.

In an attempt to find contemporary language in place of traditional theological terms such as repentance, he has introduced his own terminology, such as 'God-Expression'. As with Taylor, Peterson has expanded the text to include ideas not explicit, nor even implicit in the Greek. Joseph was righteous/just (*dikaios*), but Peterson presumes that he was 'chagrined but noble' (Matt. 1:27). Such a speculation may be acceptable in a commentary which imaginatively seeks to enlighten us on Joseph's state of mind. It is quite unjustified when it is incorporated into the text as part of Holy Writ.

Doctrinal bias may appear in his handling of 1 Corinthians 14. Texts traditionally understood as condemning homosexual conduct (1 Cor. 6:9; 1 Tim. 1:10) are translated, generalized, as 'sexual abuse'.

'Sexually confused, they abused and defiled one

another, women with women, men with men — all lust, no love.' (Rom. 1:27.)

Some might understand that Peterson leaves room for *loving* homosexual relationships. That may not of course be his intention, but the texts on homosexuality are under fire in the current climate.

John R. Kohlenberger III writes:

'Because of its interpretive and idiosyncratic nature, *The Message* should not be used for study. If read for enlightenment or entertainment, the reader should follow the advice of Augustine, as quoted in the original preface to the KJV: "Variety of translations is profitable for finding out the sense of the Scriptures".'[34]

This comment applies to any paraphrase, and indeed any translation.

The work of Peterson, Taylor, and in an earlier generation James Moffatt, illustrates both the strength and the weakness of one-translator versions. There may be a vividness, vigour and freedom in flying solo, yet there is no formal external check or control. Many writers, though by no means all, have experienced how enticing their own words can be, and how difficult it is to change the initial draft. Of course, even in committee translations, individual books are usually assigned to individual writers to produce a first draft.

Before that happens, however, the committee will have laid down clear guidelines for translators to follow. A thorough committee will test a translation both for silent reading and for reading aloud in preaching and liturgy.

Condensed versions

Is the Bible too long for the ordinary reader?

All but the most devoted readers acknowledge that some parts of the Bible are not easy going. The newcomer to the Bible may be put off by the sheer length, and be puzzled as to the benefits to be gained from genealogies, having two parallel historical accounts in Samuel-Kings and Chronicles, and other apparently repetitious passages. This is not a recent problem. It exists whenever a Bible society has to decide how much of the Scriptures it can afford to translate into a particular language. Bishop Colenso of Natal (1814-83), who was sympathetic to African traditions, questioned the value of placing in the hands of warlike people the OT stories of war and conquest. J. B. Phillips condensed the genealogies in Matthew 1 and Luke 3 in his first edition, but gave them in full in the 1958 edition.

The Dartmouth Bible. An abridgement of the King James Version, with aids to its understanding as history and literature, and as a source of religious experience was issued in 1950 and included the Apocrypha. Some might find it odd that 'a source of religious experience' is placed third, and that the expression is so vague.

The Bible designed to be read as literature was an attempt to bring the Bible to a generation that has lost contact with the Book, although the editor and arranger Ernest Sutherland Bates, could still write of Latin and Greek being taught (extensively?) in schools. The text of the AV and RV were used where thought most appropriate. Some parts of the Bible are omitted, and the whole is arranged book by book with descriptive chapter headings that do not conform to the traditional chapter divisions. Unfortunately, only a comparatively few who would not read the AV or RV were drawn to Bates' work. Bible readers already had their favourite version. Conservatives disliked the idea of cutting out any part of the Bible text.

The Reader's Digest Bible (RDB, 1972) was a serious attempt to make the Bible more accessible to the average reader. The editorial policy was not to eliminate whole books or sections, but to produce 'a text significantly shortened and clarified, yet which retains all sixty-six books, carefully preserves every incident, personality and teaching of substance; and keeps, as well, the true essence and flavor of the language'.[35] 'Condensation concerns itself with every individual word of the text, every phrase, sentence, paragraph and chapter, as well as the larger portions or blocks of text, in relation both to the theological context and the whole'.[36] The basic English text is the RSV. The layout and printing make it far more user-friendly than many versions with their double columns. There are introductions to each book, and an index of persons, places, events and teachings. This is a serious and reverent attempt to make a good translation accessible to a wider readership. The use of the RSV text ensures dignity of style, but may remain a barrier to the reader who normally gets no further than the tabloids.

The Bible in Order. All the writings which make up the Bible, arranged in their chronological order. The title speaks for itself. While not an abridgement, it is an attempt to make the Bible easier to follow. The chronological order is not necessarily the last word on the subject.

Symptomatic of the pace of modern life are books with titles including 'Minute'. There is *The One Minute Bible*, with a reading for each day. This is a set of selections, not the full Bible text. Better than nothing, but is this really the way to study the Bible? The editor has sought to meet the reality, not the ideal, when the reader would take time to read, understand and apply. The bread of life has become a snack to be taken on the run.

Bibles with extensive notes and helps
Some editions of the Bible have extensive notes to guide the reader. For example, *The New Open Bible, New*

King James Version. The Study Edition that speaks for itself. A personal Study Bible that provides a sweeping overview of Scripture and pinpoints the answers you seek and *The Dartmouth Bible* mentioned above.

The controversial notes in the *Scofield Reference Bible* (1909), and the *New Scofield Reference Bible* (1967) which use the AV text, have most effectively promoted dispensationalism.[37] As with the notes in the sixteenth-century Geneva Bible, and Archbishop Ussher's chronology in the margin of many AV printings, not every reader distinguishes between the inspired text and the uninspired notes.

The *Weston Study Bible*, with notes by Charles Gilbert Weston on the AV text, 'exposes the secret rapture, the tribulation and the millennial reign as false doctrine'.[38] The extensive notes in the study edition of the *Jerusalem Bible* are an important feature for the general reader and are both 'liberal' (historical-critical) and Catholic in tone. Layout is important in the presentation of notes, so that the biblical text is clearly differentiated from notes and commentary.

The *Thompson Chain Reference Bible* is available with the AV, NIV or NASB text. It contains a wealth of ready-made studies and outlines with a balanced and conservative approach. It is valuable for its compactness, but it is not a substitute for a good concordance, Bible dictionary and other aids. It does not interpret the text.

The Quest Study Bible has charts, maps and 200 articles giving 'fair summation of controversial passages, explanation of peculiar types of writing (like genealogies, proverbs and prophecies) . . . the over 6,000 answers . . . speak to the textual, historical and theological questions that Christians have pondered over the centuries.'[39]

The *Life Application Bible* available in five versions (NIV, LB, AV, NKJV, NRSV) has 10,000 notes. 'Each note helps you go from reading God's Word to living it.'[40]

The *Inspirational Study Bible*, contains 700 teaching units which work through five key elements from situation to exploration. There are also forty-eight topical studies by Max Lucado.

In the *Touchpoint Bible* 'you'll find a revolutionary quick reference system that steers you straight to scriptures and notes on hundreds of your greatest needs'.[41]

For those who want a number of translations in one volume, there is *The Precise Parallel New Testament*, with original Greek text and seven English translations.

Women's and other issues

The *New Inclusive Translation* seeks to use inclusive language and be 'politically correct'. David Neff notes the change from 'Son of Man' to 'Human One, child of the Father-Mother God'. The translators have lost the significance of 'Son of Man' which has strong Old Testament messianic echoes, and was Jesus' most-used name for Himself. Changing 'fellowship between light and darkness' to 'day and night' loses the rich imagery of light and darkness used especially by John.

What will we do with parts of the Bible that don't suit us? 'When an element in Scripture offends our sensibilities, it should challenge us to understand it, to reconcile ourselves to it, to correlate it with the deeper testimony of Scripture'.[42]

The *Revised English Bible* has used 'more inclusive gender references where that has been possible without compromising scholarly integrity or English style'. This avoids getting into theological minefields and losing significant resonances, as noted earlier.

The balanced approach of the NRSV is praised by Dr Aida B. Spencer:

'The NRSV is the only contemporary translation to

provide both literal meaning and inclusive language in a single translation. This keeps the NRSV closer to the original language than any other version. I recommend the NRSV to everyone because I believe English readers should know when "man" means males; "woman" means females, and "people" refers to all.'[43]

The *Women's Study Bible* uses the NKJV text and is meant for study, not devotion. There is a New Testament NRSV *Study Bible for Women* put out by Christians for Biblical Equality.

There are also Bibles addressed to the family, to children and to young people.

Minority versions

As noted earlier, it is impossible to avoid importing a degree of theological viewpoint into a translation. There are translations or annotated versions of the Bible that command minority support because of the particular perspective of the translator. Or the bias may be in the notes provided so that the faithful will correctly interpret the text.

The *New World Translation of the Holy Scriptures* (1961), published by the Watchtower (Jehovah's Witnesses) is influenced by the Witnesses' rejection of the deity of Jesus Christ. The word Jehovah is introduced into the New Testament without Greek support, and without obvious consistency. John 1:1 is translated as 'the Word was a god', influenced by doctrine, and justified by a misunderstanding of Greek grammar. Other examples could be quoted. Thomas's great confession, 'My Lord and my God' (John 20:28), has been allowed to stand. Readers of other versions will be struck by the use of 'torture stake' for cross, and 'impale' for crucify. Apart from the bias in the translation, the English is woodenly literal and lacks grace. In one way the Witnesses have done themselves no favour by putting out this translation. Doctrines that depend on a single version are hard to share with others. The prospective convert must be convinced that only one version contains the true interpretation. This point has been tacitly recognized by the Watchtower's publication of *The Bible in Living English* (1972), a translation by Steven T. Byington (1868-1957), a Congregationalist. This rather undistinguished work by a hard-working but untrained writer, uses Jehovah for LORD in the OT, perhaps its only theological attraction for the Witnesses.

All but the Church of Jesus Christ of Latter-Day Saints, or Mormon Church, reject Joseph Smith's *The Holy Scriptures: Inspired Version*, an attempt to do-over the AV to fit Mormon teaching. The book is not usually listed in works on Bible translations. Its very title indicates that it is one of a kind, not a translation in the usual sense. In Mormon missionary work it appears to play a lesser role than *The Book of Mormon*.

Versions in electronic form

This is a fast-changing market. The RSV is available as the *New Oxford Annotated Bible with Apochrypha*, for example. More details are in Chapter 10, note 8.

Choosing a translation

First, no one version should be the sole reading of the informed Christian. Translators have different aims, as has been mentioned, although all seek the glory of God. Some versions are suitable for public use, others, such as *The Amplified Bible* are not.

Some basic principles apply in choosing a translation. First, a translation should be based on the best Hebrew, Aramaic and Greek text available. Most modern translations use an eclectic text, that is a text drawn from a wide variety of sources. If you prefer to stay with the TR, or modern editions of it, your choice is narrower. Read the prefaces and notes on disputed passages, for example, Mark 16:9-20.

Secondly, the translation should be accurate, and checked by a varied group of scholars. Individual translations may be brilliant, but not wholly reliable throughout. Duthie adds that the translators should be an organized group, interdenominational, believers, with a good knowledge of the original language and culture, using the best manuscripts available with as little emendation as possible.[44] On the other hand, if the doctrinal range of the translators is too broad there is the temptation to produce a compromise text, a lowest common denominator.

Thirdly, the quality of the English is important. It should meet readers at their reading ability level, while retaining dignity, clarity, and interest. Adapting the Bible for children requires special skills in language, graphics and illustrations, so that the message is both true to the original, but comprehensible to the target age group. Unfortunately, some books of Bible stories are untrue to the plain meaning of the original. In one example, the disciples are described as waiting until the evening of the Resurrection Day without any word of what had happened. Children are entitled to the wonderful truth that the empty tomb was discovered 'very early in the morning'.

Fourthly, there are the very practical factors of durable binding, clear layout, paragraph headings and typeface, both for text and chapter and verse numbers. Personal preference will obviously play a part here. Many readers may want a more bulky study Bible for home use and a smaller Bible for church. Some study Bibles have wide margins for making notes.

Foster uses three criteria: Accuracy (both in original text and translation), Beauty and Clarity. In assessing a version he goes on to examine the theological background (for example, liberal, evangelical, RC) together with strengths, weaknesses and safeguards.[45]

Duthie asks of a translation:

First, is it translated accurately?

- Close to the original form?
- Faithful to the meaning of the original words and phrases?
- Faithful to the meaning of the original sentences?

Secondly, is the English adequate?

- How natural is the English?
- The English of today or of yesterday?
- At whose level of English is it readable?

Thirdly, is it well presented?

- Is it clear enough?
- Is it rightly divided? That is, are the divisions and sections faithful to the sense of the book?
- How accessible is it? Factors here are format, introductions, notes, cross-references, verse numbers.[46]

Duthie goes on to list the criteria by which he would evaluate a translation. Accuracy of translation accounts for 44% of the score assigned, 32% for English, 16% on presentation, and 7% for the translators, their skill in the original languages and the originals MSS used. He then proposes a nine-band ranking order: 9. GNB; 8. NJB, REB; 7. NIV; 6. NRSV, NAB2, Moffatt, LB; 5. NAB2, New Berkeley V, Revised AV, NKJV; 4. Amplified Bible.[47]

You may by now feel more confused than ever about which Bible to choose. Let me say again that no one translation is perfect, and having several Bibles to compare gives a new richness to reading and studying. For close study, the NRSV, and the NASB are hard to beat. The NIV and its revision are an excellent balance of formal and dynamic translation. Duthie places the GNB in the top rank; not all would agree. If you are a very conservative reader, yet find the AV a little difficult, the NKJV will not present you with any troubling omissions, and much of the unique beauty of the language is preserved. To get an idea of the translators' aims, read the preface to any translation that appeals to you. Check some of your favourite verses, and key texts for Christian doctrine. Bookshops are used to browsers. They hope that the longer you browse, the more you will buy. If you go to a Christian bookshop (that's where the best displays are), pick the brains of the sales staff. They will be delighted to help. Considering how much you pay for newspapers and magazines that are out-of-date within days, you can probably save up for several different Bibles.

'Let us hear the conclusion of the whole matter', a good AV sentence. No translation should be followed slavishly, not even the AV. It is helpful to draw on the insights of several translations. Some versions are valuable for devotion and freshness, but are unsound as the basis for close doctrinal study. If you read another language, you will find familiar Bible verses leaping out at you with new insights. It shows how another tongue has handled the Hebrew or Greek. As was stated earlier, no doctrine should hang on one translation alone.[48]

'The word of God is living and active.' (Heb. 4:12, NIV.)

Publishing details of the Bibles mentioned in the text are given in the Bibliography, but not in the Notes, unless there is a quotation from the Bible in the text. (Is it necessary to have full references for all the places where 'blurb' has been culled from *Christianity Today*? It's there in most places, but clogs the notes.)

[1]Metzger, Bruce; Dentan, Robert C. Harrelson, Walter. *The Making of the Revised Standard Version*. Grand Rapids, MI: Eerdmans, 1991, page 3.

[2]Moffatt, Introduction to *A New Translation of the Bible*, London: Hodder & Stoughton, 1935, page xliv.

[3]Moffatt, pages xliv, xlv.

[4]Lewis Foster, *Selecting a Translation of the Bible*, Cincinnati, OH: Standard Publishing, 1983, pages 98, 99.

[5]Foster, *Selecting*, pages 99-100.

[6]'A heretical, communist inspired Bible', Metzger 1991, page 51; Bruce, *History*, pages 194-2007.

[7]Kubo, page 97.

[8]Dennis Nineham, ed. *The New English Bible Reviewed*, London: Epworth, 1965, page ix.

[9]NEB, Introduction to the New Testament, page vii.

[10]IDB, Supplementary vol., page 933.

[11]Nineham, pages 143-144.

[12]Terence H. Brown in Nineham, page 144.

[13]Frank W. Beare in Nineham, page 13.

[14]Nineham, pages 143-151.

[15]Nineham, page 152.

[16]Preface to the NKJV, pages iii, v.

[17]As advertised in *Christianity Today* 39/14 (Dec. 1995), page 74.

[18]Preface to the NIV, pages vi, viii.

[19]Kubo, page 259.

[20]Boone, page 48.

[21]Preface to the NIV, pages vi, vii.

[22]Kenneth L. Barker, *The Making of a Contemporary Translation, The New International Version*, London: Hodder & Stoughton, 1987.

[23]'The *New International Version* on the Prologue of John', *Harvard Theological Review* 172 (1979), pages 305-310.

[24]Steve Chalke wrote the Introduction to the NIrV, which is quoted in the promotional material.

[25]Quoted in promotional material, as above.

[26]Kubo, page 223.

[27]From the advertisement in *Christianity Today* 39/4 (3 April 1995), Advert. section, pages 4, 8; Barclay M. Newman, 'A Message in terms most people can understand', *Bible Translator* (Practical papers) (April 1996), 47:201-207. Newman headed the team that prepared the CEV.

[28]God's Word, Angel Bible.

[29]IDB Supplementary vol., page 935.

[30]Kubo, page 61.

[31]Preface to the *Living Bible*, np. Taylor is aware of the strengths and pitfalls of paraphrases.

[32]John Wilson, 'The Living Bible Reborn', *Christianity Today*, 40: (Oct. 1996), pages 33-35.

[33]in Kubo, pages 162, 163.

[34]Kohlenberger, 'Bible paraphrases — their possibilities and perils' *Christian Research Journal*, Spring/Summer 1994.

[35]Kubo, page 310.

[36]Kubo, page 310; Preface to the RDB, page ix.

[37]Cyrus I. Scofield (1843-1921, EDT.), page 988.

[38]Clifton Book Co. Advertised in *Christianity Today* 39/11 (Sept. 1995), page 66.

[39]*The Quest Study Bible*, NIV. Advertised in *Christianity Today* 39/9 (14 August 1995), page 11.

[40]Life Application Bible, *Christianity Today*, Bible Reference Update (Fall 1995), page 9.

[41]Touchpoint Bible, *Christianity Today* 40/13 (Nov. 1996), page 7.

[42]Editorial, *Christianity Today*, 39/2 (Feb. 1995), page 19.

[43]Aida Besançon Spencer on NRSV, *Christianity Today* 40/19 (Oct. 1996), page 79.

[44]Duthie, page 181.

[45]Foster, *Selecting*, pages 64, 86-125.

[46]Duthie, pages 172-177.

[47]Duthie, 'an Order of Merit' pages 191-208. Only the more commonly-available versions have been included from Duthie's extensive list.

[48]For an annotated list of Bible translations from 1900-82, Kubo, pages 345-375; For 'a chronology of representative English translations from Wyclif to the present' (1960), Beegle, pages 121, 122. Foster critiques the AV, NASB, NEB, RSV, GNB, LB, NIV, JB, and NKJV. The most recent survey is Duthie.

CHAPTER TEN

'And is profitable . . . '

2 Timothy 3:16

A unique set of books

Christians believe that the Bible is like no other book. The non-Christian may look at a black leather-bound volume, printed in two columns and divided, not only into chapters, but broken up into little bits called verses. Christians sometimes appear to pick out verses apparently from here and there and quote them as authority. This will not sound quite so strange if one has heard how the Koran is used, or at one time the little red book of Chairman Mao's sayings. But it may not be the best way to use the Bible. However, the Bible is not a talisman to be kept in the home, a sign of respectability and good taste, a good thing to have, but not for reading.

Both the New and Old Testaments were written in an oral rather than a written culture. Jeremiah, Paul, and probably others dictated and a secretary, or amanuensis, took down the words. You can almost hear Paul thinking aloud as he tries to remember whom he baptized in Corinth (Rom. 1:22; Col. 4:18; 1 Cor. 1:14-16). Most of the early Christians would have heard the Bible rather than read it. The letter to the Romans must have required close attention, but we can imagine that the reader was interrupted by questions, and went over the reading again and made it clear before going further.

Reading aloud

Silent reading is comparatively modern. Reading aloud takes time. When you see a reader's lips moving you know that this is not speed reading. But some parts of the Bible cry out to be read aloud, or sung. The Psalms may be best appreciated when we actually mouth them, when the words become audible, and the range of emotions finds voice. Reading aloud helps us to throw ourselves into the feeling of the inspired writer, to share the thrill of the experience with God, to repeat the words given by the Lord, to tell of heights and depths of experience.

The *Dramatised Bible* assigns parts to the various speakers, for example, Jesus, the narrator, the disciples, the crowd, and is wonderful for group reading. The various readers can put themselves into their parts more easily than one reader who has to read the whole passage and assume every role.

Looking inside

The sixty six books include

Narratives — stories, histories.

Prophecies, which may be divided into two groups: the major and twelve minor prophets of the OT, and the apocalyptic prophecies of Daniel and the Revelation which focus on the cosmic struggle and the end of time when God's kingdom will be finally established.

Poetry. The AV prints poetry as prose, not giving clear line breaks. Many translations from the RV on have separated the lines, setting out the poetry in verse form. Ideally, each line of poetry should occupy one line of print which can be done when a whole-page (for example in the JB) rather than two-column format is used. Poetry in both the Old and New Testament will be considered in more detail later in this chapter.

Gospels. These are not biographies in the modern sense, but a telling of the good news of Jesus Christ.

Letters (epistles).

All these types have a purpose, and of course they are

not rigidly separated. Isaiah, for example, has both narrative and prophecy, and prose and verse.

Where to start?

I'm new to the Bible. Where should I start? Try 'the report of the Good News', the story of Jesus as told by Mark, probably for a Gentile audience, perhaps in Rome. Settle down and read the story at one go. It takes about an hour and a half to read aloud. Richard Burridge likens Mark's Jesus to a lion, symbolism that goes back to Jerome, who drew on Ezekiel 1:4-28 and Revelation 4:7.[1] Mark's Jesus suddenly appears as a grown man, without any Christmas story. The narrative is fast-paced, urgent, and vivid, especially in the AV and other versions that translate every word.

Then you can look at the parallel gospels of Matthew and Luke. Matthew, the Teacher of Israel, emphasizes the fulfilment of OT prophecy. Jesus is the Messiah. Luke, symbolized as the ox, the Bearer of burdens, by Jerome, addresses his work to Theophilus. Luke's gospel and Acts are an excellent bridge to the Gentile world. Matthew and Mark, together with Luke, are called Synoptic gospels because they all share the basic framework of Mark and include almost all he wrote. However, the careful reader will see that all three writers have their special emphases. They don't completely 'see eye to eye' as 'Synoptic' might imply. They complement each other without contradicting. The Holy Spirit guided the gospel writers to target particular audiences and meet their needs.

John

The gospel of John, showing us Jesus the soaring eagle, has a quite different atmosphere. He echoes Genesis, 'In the beginning', and confronts us with the mystery: 'The Word was made flesh, and lived among us, and we saw his glory . . . full of grace and truth.' Here there are no parables in the usual sense; there are long speeches from Jesus not found elsewhere; and miracles are called 'signs'. There is no breaking of bread in the upper room, but there is a service of foot washing. We need all four gospels together to complete the portrait of the Lord. Some suggest that John's gospel is the place to begin, and give his book to enquirers. Others give Mark. There is no right or wrong way. God has different ways to the heart.

The same, yet different

It is fascinating to read accounts of the same incident in the life of Jesus as recorded in two, three or four gospel accounts. You may be startled or even disturbed by the fact that events do not always occur in the same order, for instance the temptations in Matthew 4:1-10 and Luke 4:1-12. The denials of Peter and the post-resurrection appearance of our Lord are not easy to fit into a framework. Dialogues differ in what must be the same story, the transfiguration and the demon possessed boy (Matt. 17:1-21; Mark 9:2-29; Luke 9:28-42). This is no cause for distress. As one writer put it, 'The Lord gave His word in just the way He wanted it to come. He gave it through different writers, each having his own individuality, though going over the same history.' We can leave the technical puzzles to the scholars and enjoy the richness of seeing the same story from differing and complementary angles, four portraits of Jesus. Do you remember the Van Dyck portrait of Charles I, two profiles and one full face? I feel I understand a little more about the man behind that pensive face because I can study him from three aspects.

After you have looked at the life of Jesus, you could move on to read the Acts of the Apostles (the acts of the Holy Spirit through the apostles). This will introduce you to Paul, give you a new view of Peter, and prepare the way for reading their letters.

The Old Testament

By this time you will have seen repeated references to the Old Testament, so if this is unfamiliar territory, it may be time to explore, beginning at Genesis. Parts of Leviticus and Numbers you may find hard going. You don't have to plough doggedly through genealogies. They are there for a purpose, but may not be helpful to you. You are reading for understanding and blessing, not as a labour of piety or good works. There are some books that can be read without knowing anything about the historical background, even though this is always

---

The Old Testament in three parts

Law (Torah) *the five books of Moses:* Genesis to Deuteronomy.

Prophets: *Former Prophets:* Joshua, Judges, Samuel, Kings.

Latter Prophets: Isaiah, Jeremiah, Ezekiel, the twelve minor prophets.

Writings: The writings included all the books not in the first two categories.

Poetry: Psalms, Proverbs, Job.

The Five Scrolls: Song of Solomon, Ruth, Lamentations, Ecclesiastes, Esther.

Prophecy: Daniel.

History: Ezra-Nehemiah, 1-2 Chronicles.

This helps us to understand references in the NT to 'the law and the prophets'.

helpful: Job, Psalms, Proverbs, Ecclesiastes, Song of Solomon.

Verrecchia suggests another possible route:

Introduction: Genesis, Exodus, Joshua.

Prophets and Kings: 1 and 2 Samuel, 1 and 2 Kings, Amos, Micah.

The time of reconstruction: Ezra, Nehemiah, Esther.

The time of Messiah: Mark.

The time of the church: Acts of the Apostles, Epistles.

The time of maturity and encounter: Gospel of John.[2]

Daniel is the fullest example of the type of writing known as *apocalyptic:* the unveiling of things to come, kept secret up to that time. It concerns the future more than the present, the spiritual world rather than the material, and God will intervene in the course of history. Some of Daniel's imagery is echoed in the Revelation or Apocalypse. Daniel wrote during the seventy-year exile, prophesying the rebuilding of Jerusalem and an ultimate destruction of evil.[3] The 'Son of Man', who received dominion and glory and kingdom, is the name Jesus used most often for Himself. No one doubted its significance when, on trial for His life, Jesus declared that they would 'see the Son of man sitting at the right hand of Power' (Mark 14:61, 62). Daniel's time prophecies have fascinated readers over the centuries. Many have understood the 'seventy-sevens' or seventy weeks to indicate the date of Messiah's ministry (Dan. 9:25).

Poetry

Any good Bible dictionary or commentary on the Psalms will introduce you to Hebrew poetic writing. This will enrich the understanding of why the writers said it the way they did. Since the Bible is being read in translation we must look for the poetry in the play of ideas rather than in the rhythms and word-play of the Hebrew original. Today we tend to regard the pun as low-level wit, but the Hebrew prophets used it with great effect. It was not out of place in messages from the Lord, and Jesus himself used these literary arts.

Hebrew poetry in the Bible, especially in the Psalms, runs the whole range of emotions and experiences, assuring us that others have shared our joys and sorrow, our shouts of joy, and howls of pain and despair, finding hope in God at the last.

The following is just a taster of the structure of both Old and New Testament poetry. Hebrew poetry, as found in the Psalms and many other books, is written in two or three lines which run parallel to each other.

For example:
'Thy word is a lamp unto my feet,
and a light unto my path.' (Ps. 119:105, AV.)

This is *synonymous* parallelism, as shown again in:
'LORD, who may dwell in your sanctuary?
Who may live on your holy hill?' (Ps. 15:1, NIV.)

Contrasting, or *antithetic* parallelism is:
'For the LORD watches over the way of the
righteous,
but the way of the wicked will perish.' (Ps. 1:6, NIV.)

Notice the build up of ideas in the following example of progressive or *climactic* or progressive parallelism:
'The LORD is in his holy temple;
the LORD is on his heavenly throne.
He observes the sons of men;
his eyes examine them.' (Ps. 11:4, NIV.)

Luke introduces three poetic speeches, which for centuries have been used as part of the liturgy: The song of Mary, the Magnificat, so called from the first word of the Latin version (Luke 1:46-55); the Benedictus, the prophecy of Zechariah at the naming of the infant John the Baptist (Luke 1:68-79); and the grateful prayer, the Nunc Dimittis, of Simeon as he held the infant Redeemer (Luke 2:29-32). Only Luke relates these hymns. Could it be that Mary 'kept all these sayings in her heart' and later related them to Luke or to one of the sources from which he composed his gospel? (Luke 1:1-4; 2:51.)

Mary's song, which echoes that of Hannah (1 Sam. 2:1-10), but is more profound, begins with synonymous parallelism.[4]

'My soul doth magnify the Lord,
and my spirit hath rejoiced in God my Saviour.'

Contrasting, or antithetical parallel thoughts are:
'He hath put down the mighty from their seats,
and exalted them of low degree.
He hath filled the hungry with good things;
and the rich he hath sent empty away.'

Simeon's song concludes with:
'A light to lighten the Gentiles,
and the glory of thy people Israel.'

The two lines are parallel, but the thought contrasts 'light', and 'glory'.

Hugh Schonfield suggests that the opening words of John's gospel were an antiphonal hymn interspersed with brief remarks. These are indicated by the italics here:
'In the beginning was the Word
And the Word was with God
So the Word was Divine
He was in the beginning with God
By him everything had being
And without him nothing had being.
What had being by him was Life
And Life was the Light of men

And the Light shines in the Darkness
  And the Darkness could not suppress it.'

'This was the true Light
  It illumines all who enter the world
He was in the world, (and the world had being by
      him)
  But the world did not recognize him
He came to his own domain
  And his own did not receive him.'
      (John 1:1-11.)[5]

The line structure of Jesus' many pithy sayings is clear. Our Lord had characteristic ways of speaking, including contrasting (antithetic) parallelism:

'So, if your eye is sound, your whole body will be
    full of light
But if your eye is not sound, your whole body
    will be full of darkness.'
    (Matt. 6:22b-23a.)

'Every good tree brings forth good fruits
But the corrupt tree brings forth evil fruits.'
    (Matt. 7:17.)

There are also examples where the two lines say the same thing in different ways:

'for he (your Father) makes his sun rise on the evil
    and on the good,
and sends rain on the just and on the unjust.'
    (Matt. 5:45.)

Other examples of poetic form are given by Schonfield:
  A. 'Do not judge, and you will not be judged.'
  A. 'Do not condemn, and you will not be
      condemned.'

    B. 'For the judgment you pass will be passed on
       you.'
    B. 'And the measure you use will be used on you.'

    A. 'Do not offer gems to the dogs.'
    B. 'Or they may turn and rend you.'
    A. 'Nor strew your pearls before pigs.'
    B. 'Or they may trample you underfoot.'
        (Matt. 7:1, 2, 6.)

In these examples, the A lines have a similar meaning
(synonymous parallelism), and the B pair show the consequences.[6]

Such careful and effective use of words makes us
realize that Jesus did not just stand up and speak. The
long hours of prayer and meditation probably included
planning His talk. The fact that Jesus spoke in a such a
memorable way meant that His hearers were able to
preserve the tradition, to be passed down to the reader
today.[7]

Paul records, or wrote, two examples of what are considered early Christian hymns and statements of belief:
Philippians 2:6-11, 1 Timothy 3:16. The NIV, JB and some
other translations print these in verse form.

Seeking to understand: a case study
1. What the prophet meant then
What do we know about the writer?

What was the background, his life and times?

Are we told why the message was given or the story
told? The prophets make it clear that they had to speak
'the word of the Lord'.

What did the writing mean at the time it was written?
Let us look at an example.

The year is about 760 BC, the place Bethel town in
Israel, the Northern kingdom. Amos, not a professional

prophet, but a shepherd called by the Lord, is a new voice
on the street, and he is telling of all the bad things that
will happen to six heathen nations because of what they
have done. 'Amen! Hear! Hear! Preach on!', the crowd
encourages. The heathen deserve all they get. Then Amos
starts on Judah, closer home, but the northerners think
the Judean southerners are a self-righteous bunch who
really need taking down a peg. Seven prophecies of
trouble — the perfect number. But he hasn't finished.
Now Amos brings it right home, to Israel, to Bethel, with
the longest speech of the eight. And even then he is not
finished. Their religion is a mockery. Social injustice and
oppression are rife, and the Lord will send judgement. No
wonder the authorities expel him. And in the south Isaiah
has the same message, for example in chapter 58. God
hates religion without social justice.

2. **What the prophet says to us today**

What does Amos say today? The problems of Amos's
time have not gone away. There is still social injustice,
still self-deception, still religion that is a mockery of
God's character.

How does it apply to me? Yes, I admit there are many
things wrong with the world. It's a shame. Yes, and now
what am I going to do about it, starting with God and me?
How do I look in relation to what the Lord said through
Amos? What can I do to set my own house in order,
before trying to clean up the neighbourhood, the
country, the Church and the world? Amos does not end
in gloom. The Lord promises restoration. There are
conditions, but there is a sure hope.

It may help me to see how God led His people in the
time of Amos, and will do the same today.

It may help me to see that God is in control and so sin
and suffering will one day come to an end at the 'day of
the Lord'.

It may help me to see God's viewpoint on social evils,
as we compare His ideals with the way His people fell
short and still do. We then have to decide what action we
should take to deal with bad situations: oppression both
economic and political, intolerance, persecution, hatred,
alienation.

It may help me to see changes God needs to make in my
own life to make me truly Christian, which is to be
Christlike. This may mean changes in lifestyle, career,
spending patterns, personal relationships at home, at
work and socially. The Bible is a mirror, and we need to
act on what we see (James 1:22-25).

Bible reading and prayer

The Bible should be read with a prayer that God will
give us understanding and appreciation. We ask the same
Holy Spirit who inspired the Scriptures to guide us as we
read. Is our conscience subject to the Word of God, as
Luther put it, or do we search the Scriptures to find
support for our own views? It must be accepted as the
word from the *Lord*, admittedly served in an earthenware
container.

As we read, subjects for prayer will present themselves.
Then, as we pray, Bible promises are there for us to present to the Lord in faith. So there is an inextricable
relationship between Bible reading and prayer. Neither is
complete without the other. Read with pencil and paper.
Write down the insights you receive.

Ideas for reading and study

The type of reading you plan may influence which
translation you use. For devotion a paraphrase may
express the thought of the Bible writer very vividly,
though not always exactly. When you wish to study more

closely just what is meant, then you need a different type of version.

Biographies. Sometimes the story is told in one place, Samson's for example. If you want to follow through Peter's story you will need to look at all four gospels, Acts, and Peter's two letters. Some background reading will help to make the story more understandable.

Word studies, where an idea, such as 'grace', 'love', 'judgement', is followed through both Testaments.

Themes such as the second coming.

Helps

By now it's become clear that we need some extra resources if we are to get the most out of our Bible study.

First, a good concordance. For the AV, Young, *Analytical Concordance* gives more help than Strong in studying the usage of Hebrew and Greek words. Strong, *Exhaustive Concordance* (various editions) gives every word in the AV and RV, with Hebrew, Aramaic and Greek originals. It indicates by numbers which underlying word is being used. You can then turn up the word by number and find its meaning. Buy a version that does not include all the articles and prepositions. This will be cheaper, and easier to handle. The number system in Strong is used on several reference systems, for example, *Theological Wordbook of the Old Testament* and some computer programs. Strong may therefore be more useful than Young in this respect.

Have a look at both Strong and Young before deciding which suits you best. Cruden's concordance is a blunt instrument compared with these. It does not distinguish between different words translated by the same word in English. For example, Image (AV) translates two Greek words, and may be misused to try to prove that Christ is a created being (Col. 1:15; 2 Cor. 4:4).

John the Baptist was not the light (phos = light) (John 1:8), but he was 'a burning and shining light' (luchnos = lamp) (John 5:35). Some translations make the distinction.

Another potential trap with concordance searches using only Cruden is that the same Hebrew, Aramaic or Greek word may not be consistently translated into English. The good reason for this is that words vary in meaning according to context, and therefore a wooden word-for-word translation without reference to context would not give the true sense. The bad reason for inconsistency is that translators, including the AV, sometimes used different English words for the same original without good reason. Just and righteous as used by Paul are not two ideas, but one (*dikaios*).

When buying a concordance, make sure that it is one designed for your translation. It is frustrating to use Young or Strong with the NIV, for example.

Electronic concordances

There are several programmes you can run on a PC or AppleMac. These will clearly save a great deal of time as you can transfer text from the program on to your own study. Logos 2 is perhaps the most comprehensive and is available at four levels, including study and devotional helps.[8]

Bible commentaries

Commentaries may serve a number of purposes: textual, grammatical/linguistic, historical background, exegetical (explaining the meaning), homiletical (drawing lessons from the text for devotion or preaching).

Before buying a commentary, decide what you want from it: theologically liberal or conservative, what denominational background, technical or non-technical.

Will discussion of the Hebrew and Greek text benefit or bother you? The best for the average reader are those that explain what the text in the original languages has to say, without assuming that we know the language. Look inside before you buy. Find out what friends recommend and use.

A basic decision is between buying a complete set, or selecting commentaries from different sources, choosing the best for our purposes on individual books. In a series the quality of individual volumes may vary, though buying a second-hand whole set can sometimes be a bargain.

William Barclay's commentary series on the New Testament is evangelically and scholastically sound, well suited for those who want a devotional commentary.

Tyndale Old Testament Commentaries/New Testament Commentaries, Inter-Varsity Press. Everything coming from this press is conservative.

Using a commentary

Read the Bible first, interrogate the text and squeeze all you can out of it before going to the commentary. It is too easy to let someone else do the thinking for us. Keep asking questions. Who said it? How? Why? When? Where? How you interrogate the text will depend on the type of Bible passage you are examining. Then go to the commentary with questions. You don't have to agree with the commentary. As with fruit, you throw out the pith and the pips. Having several commentaries helps to keep a balance, though it is expensive.

Bible Dictionaries, like commentaries, come with different perspectives along the spectrum from historical-critical to conservative. For example, are Abraham, Moses, the Exodus, David accepted as historical figures or events according to the Bible account?

Let me say it again. Before buying aids to Bible study, browse through catalogues and your local Christian bookshops, talk to the sales persons and pick their brains. In the end, it's up to you to choose something that you find user-friendly, yet with enough challenge to stretch you.

Personal needs

The Holy Spirit and prayer. The Bible should never be studied without prayer. It's worth repeating. In order to fathom the riches of the Bible we need the help of the same Holy Spirit who inspired it.

Time. Always in short supply, but there is no substitute.

Reverent curiosity. We learn by asking questions. That is what the disciples did.

What is the biblical background, that is, the context of the passage?

What happens in your passage, and how does it relate to the background?

Who are the actors/speakers?

Why do you think God wished the incident to be recorded?

What would the passage have meant to contemporaries?

What does it mean to you today? How can you make your understanding meaningful to others, your children, your friends, a church group?

Does the passage speak to you with enough force that you feel urged to do something about it?

Have I really understood what was/is going on? Remember my Latin teacher, 'Caesar did not write nonsense.' Nor did Bible writers write nonsense. The careless reader may sometimes make nonsense of parts of the Bible. There is a story of an earnest soul who examined a hair under a microscope and was puzzled because he could not see the number (Matt. 10:30), or quote poetical passages to prove that the earth is flat. One person I knew of had a Bible that had fallen to pieces, the pages jumbled up. But for him, the order/disorder was divinely ordained. Ridiculous and short-lived interpretations are given to current events, for example, Hitler's flying bombs, the doodlebugs were said by a zealot to be a fulfilment of the flying roll (Zech. 5:1). No wonder the Lord invited us to 'reason together', 'argue it out' (Isa. 1:18, AV, NEB).

Read a variety of translations, but recognize the limitations of each. Augustine of Hippo wrote, 'Confronting different translations, makes it possible, by feeling one's way, to perceive something of the original towards which they converge, even for the reader for whom the original remains inaccessible'.[9]

Other languages. Read the Bible in any foreign language you know. Reading another language helps to point out things not noticed in a too-familiar text. Most of us read a second or third language more slowly than the mother tongue. The mental effort helps us concentrate, and sometimes hitherto unnoticed points come to view.

Mark mentions 'the centurion, which stood over against Jesus' (Mark 15:39). The significance hit me one morning as I read the story in Swedish, my wife's mother tongue. The centurion was facing Jesus. Isn't facing Jesus what leads us to say, 'Truly this man *is* — no longer merely *was* — the Son of God'? Of course, if I had been more alert I should have figured out the meaning (it is quite clear in the NIV), but I had in mind pictures of the crucifixion where the centurion stands alongside the cross, looking straight ahead. A fixed idea obscured the text.

A balanced approach. It is unsafe to build a belief or

doctrine on a single text or part of a text. For example, Luke 12:22 is translated 'Take no thought' (AV); 'Do not be anxious' (RSV), 'do not worry' (NIV). The AV might suggest fatalism, or inactivity. The real meaning is, do not worry, take no *anxious* thought.

'Drink ye all of it' (AV), or 'Drink of it, all of you' (RSV), 'Drink from it all of you' (NIV), (Matt. 26:27). Did Jesus mean that each disciple should drink, or that the whole cup must be emptied? The AV is perhaps unclear to the modern reader, although the original language is clear that all should drink.

'At the name of Jesus every knee should bow.' Is that a command for now, or a promise of what will come? (Phil. 2:10.)

If one uses a calculator without any feel for numbers there is no check on the answer. Results are checked against experience. So with the Scriptures. Experience helps us to make sense. A word/phrase strikes you. Compare scripture with scripture to see if the idea holds up. A text out of context may serve as pretext, not a basis for faith and practice.

'The Bible was given for practical purposes', a guide to life and the way to eternal life. It is the record of God's dealings with His creation. It challenges the intellect, and the emotions. It is a call to respond to the love of God revealed through the life of

'Jesus Christ His only Son our Lord,
 Who was conceived by the Holy Ghost,
 Born of the Virgin Mary,
 Suffered under Pontius Pilate,
 Was crucified, dead and buried,
 He descended into the grave;
 The third day He rose again from the dead,
 He ascended into heaven,
 And sits on the right hand of God the Father Almighty;

From thence He shall come to judge the living and the dead.'

It is the writer's prayer that as you read your Bible you will come to know Jesus personally. To know Him is to have everlasting life (John 17:3).

---

[1]Richard Burridge, *Four Gospels, One Jesus?*, London: SPCK, 1994, page 33.
[2]Verrecchia, page 50.
[3]Most critics place Daniel in the time of Antiochus Epiphanes (reigned 175-164 BC), and see that very real but temporary menace as the evil power denoted by, for example, the 'little horn' (Daniel 7:8, 20, 21). Conservative scholars point out that Jesus referred to Daniel's prediction of a mysterious event yet to come (Matt. 24:15). The notable Anglo-Catholic E. B. Pusey (1800-82) in *Daniel the Prophet*, Oxford, 1864, asserted the messianic fulfilment of the seventy weeks' prophecy.
[4]The names are taken from the opening word in Latin.
[5]Hugh J. Schonfield, *The Authentic New Testament, edited and translated from the Greek for the general reader*, London: Dennis Dobson, 1956, pages 451, 452.
[6]Schonfield, page 62.
[7]Jeremias, *New Testament* 8-29.
[8]Sunrise Software, Scorrier Park, Scorrier, Cornwall, TR16 5AU, produce a full-colour catalogue. Tel: (01209) 821821; Fax: (01209) 822125.

Logos 2 is published in the UK by Hodder and Stoughton, 47 Bedford Sq., London, WC1B 3DP. Tel: (0171) 636 9851; Fax: (0171) 631 5248, who also publish BibleMaster, a less ambitious program.

The Franklin Bookman is available in the NIV440/KJB440 New International/King James Bible (Size: 120x83x14mm) or the 640 which has the same capabilities but larger in size (140x100x25mm). The facilities include complete Bible text, spell correction, footnotes, comprehensive concordance, word/phrase search. The Bookman comes with either AV or NIV installed, but you can change versions by inserting a different cartridge. Franklin Electronic Publishers (UK) Ltd, 7 Windmill Business Village, Brooklands Close, Sunbury-on-Thames, Middlesex, TW16 7DY. Tel: (01932) 770185; Fax: (01932) 772773. The Bookman is clearly not a substitute for more powerful programs, but fits a pocket or brief case.

The *Biblical Archaeology Review*, Nov/Dec 1996, pages 59-66, 75, has a feature comparison of sixteen Bible software programs. These are divided into three categories: for those familiar with Hebrew and Greek; for those who want access to the original languages, but not at a scholarly level; and thirdly, for those speaking only English. There are also four Christian Web sites. Before investing, decide the level at which you wish to operate, do some research and ask users for their experience. See if you can get some hands-on experience before making a decision.

Christianity Today issues a spring and autumn 'Bible Reference Update' which keeps abreast of the fast-moving scene.

[9]*Parole Vivante*, page 10.

Select Bibliography

Bible versions: This is not a complete list of translations into English, and omits some of those out-of-print or not currently advertised.

AMP: *The Amplified Bible*, Grand Rapids, MI: Zondervan, 1965.

AV: *Authorized Version* or King James Version, 1611.

BIO: *Bible, The, in Order. All the Writings which make up the Bible, arranged in their chronological order*, ed. by Jospeh Rhymer, London: Darton, Longman and Todd, 1975.

BIOY: *The Bible in One Year*, NIV, London: Hodder & Stoughton, 1988.

CDR: *Cambridge Daily Reading Bible*, NRSV. Daily readings to cover the whole Bible over two years. Cambridge: Cambridge University Press, 1995.

CEV: *The Contemporary English Version/Bible for Today's Family*, New York: American Bible Society; Nashville, TN: Thomas Nelson, 1995. Also published as *The Promise*.

DaB: *Bible, The, Dartmouth. An abridgement of the King James Version, with aids to its understanding as history and literature, and as a source of religious experience*. Includes Apochrypha. Ray B. Chamberlin, Herman Feldman. Boston: Houghton Miflin, 1950.

DB: *The Dramatized Bible*, edited by Michael Perry, London: Marshall Pickering, 1988.

EDB: See *New Century Version*.

GWAB: *God's Word Angel Bible*, Grandville, MI: World Publishing, 1996.

GNB: *Good New Bible*, or Today's English Version, 1946, 1952, 1971, 1973.

HGSB: *Hebrew Greek Study Bible*, Chattanooga, TN: AMG Publishers. NIV text.

ISB: *Inspirational Study Bible*, ed. Max Lucado, Dallas, TX: Word. In the NCV/EDB text.

JB: *The Jerusalem Bible*, London: Darton Longman & Todd, 1966. Used by permission of the publisher.

LAB: *Life Application Bible*, NIV. Wheaton, IL: Tyndale, 1989.

LBP: *The Living Bible Paraphrased*, Kenneth N. Taylor, Wheaton, IL: Tyndale House, 1971.

NASB: *The New American Standard Bible*, La Habra, CA: The Lockman Foundation 1960, 1962, 1963, 1968, 1971, 1973, 1975, 1977. Updated NASB, *Christianity Today* 40/11 (Oct. 1996, page 17).

NCV: *New Century Version*, Nashville, TN: Thomas Nelson, 1988.

NEB: *The New English Bible*, c. The delegates of the Oxford University Press and the Syndics of the Cambridge University Press, 1961, 1970.

NGSB: The *New Geneva Study Bible*, Nashville, TN: Thomas Nelson.

NIV: The Holy Bible: *New International Version*, New York: International Bible Society, 1978; London: Hodder & Stoughton, 1979. The NIV now appears in various forms: The New Adventure Bible, Teen Study Bible, Student Bible, The Quest (see separate entry), Full Life Study Bible, NIV Study Bible.

NJB. *New Jerusalem Bible*, London: Darton, Longman and Todd, 1985.

NKJV: *The New King James Version*, Nashville, TN: Thomas Nelson, 1982. Also issued as *Spirit Filled Life Bible*.

NLT: *Holy Bible: New Living Translation*, Wheaton, IL: Tyndale, 1995.

NOB: *New Open Bible, New King James Version. The Study Edition that speaks for itself. A personal Study Bible that provides a sweeping overview of Scripture and pinpoints the answers you seek*. Nashville, TN: Thomas Nelson, 1990.

NSB: *New Student Bible*, Christianity Today, NIV text. See *Christianity Today* 40/12 (9 Dec. 1996) page 16.

OMB: *The One-Minute Bible*, ed. John Kohlenberger III. Bloomington, MN: Garborg's Heart n Home, 1992. This gives a selected passage for each day. Does not include the complete text.

OYB: *One Year Bible*, Wheaton, IL: Tyndale House. Complete text in 365 15-minute portions. Various versions available 1985 on.

PPNT: *The Precise Parallel New Testament*, Oxford: Oxford University Press, 1996. Texts: Greek, AV, Rheims, AMP, NIV, NRSV, NAB, NASB.

QSB: *The Quest Study Bible*, NIV, 1995. Advertised in *Christianity Today* 39/9 (14 August 1995), page 11.

REB: *The Revised English Bible*, Oxford & Cambridge (as NEB), 1989.

RSB: *Ryrie Study Bible*, Chicago: Moody Press, 1995.

RSV: *Revised Standard Version* of the Bible, copyrighted 1946, 1952, 1971, 1973.

SBW: *Study Bible for Women*, NT, RSV, Grand Rapids, MI, Baker Book House.

SRVCV: *Holy Bible: Standard Revised Version Catholic Version*, Princeton, NJ: Scepter Publications.

TCR: *Thompson Chain Reference Bible*, Indianapolis, IN: Kirkbride Bible Co. In AV, NIV, or NASB.

TEV: *The Everyday Bible* see *New Century Version*.

TPB: The *Touchpoint Bible*, Wheaton, IL: Tyndale House. NLT text *The Promise, Contemporary English Version* See CEV above.

21: *Twenty-first/21st Century King James Version*, Gary, SD: KJ21 Publishers.

WSB: *Weston Study Bible*, Clifton Book Company. Full

details not traced. Advertised in Christianity Today 39/9 (11 Sept. 1995), page 66.

WomSB: *Women's Study Bible*, Nashville, TN, Thomas Nelson, 1995.

Books, periodicals, pamphlets

Anderson, G. W. and other TBS publications are listed under Trinitarian Bible Society.

Barker, Kenneth L., *The making of a contemporary translation, The New International Version*, London: Hodder & Stoughton, 1987.

Beegle, Dewer M., *God's Word into English.* New York: Harper, 1960.

Betteridge, Maurice S., 'The Bitter Notes: The Geneva Bible and its Annotations'. *The Sixteenth Century Journal*, XLV.1 (Spring 1983), pages 41-62 (62).

Blomberg, Craig L., *Interpreting the Parables*, Leicester: Apollos, 1990.

Bosworth, James, *The Gospels: Gothic, Anglo-Saxon, Wycliffe and Tyndale Versions*, London, 1907.

Boone, Kathleen C. Boone, *The Bible Tells Them So: the Discourse of Protestant Fundamentalism*, London, SCM, 1990.

Brown, Colin, *New International Dictionary of New Testament Theology*, Grand Rapids, MI: Zondervan.

Bruce, F. F., *History of the Bible in English*, Guildford: Lutterworth, 1971.

Burgon: Burgon, J. W., *The Revised Version*, London: John Murray, 1883.

Burridge, Richard A., *Four Gospels, One Jesus?*, London: SPCK, 1994.

Carson, D. A., *Exegetical Fallacies*, Grand Rapids, MI: Baker Book House, 1984.

——, *The King James Version Debate* Grand Rapids, MI: Baker Book House, 1993.

Comfort, Philip Wesley, *The Quest for the Original Text of the New Testament*, Grand Rapids, MI: Baker Book House, 1992.

Dictionary of New Testament Theology, 3 vols., ed. Colin Brown, Grand Rapids, MI: Zondervan; Exeter: Paternoster Press, 1978.

Duthie, Alan S., *How to choose your Bible wisely*, Carlisle: Paternoster Press; Swindon: Bible Society, 1995.

Ehrman, Bart D., *The Orthodox Corruption of Scripture: The Effects of Early Christological Controversies on the Text of the New Testament*, New York, Oxford: Oxford University Press, 1993.

Epp, E. J. and Fee, G. D., *Studies in the Theory and Method of New Testament Criticism*, Grand Rapids, MI: Eerdmans, 1993.

Evangelical Dictionary of Theology, ed. Walter A. Elwell, Grand Rapids, MI: Baker Book House, 1984.

Expositor's Bible Commentary, Grand Rapids, MI: Zondervan, vol. 8, 1984, vol. 9, 1981.

Farstad, Arthur L. and Hodges, Zance C., eds. *The Greek New Testament Majority Text*, Nelson, 1982.

Fee, Gordon D., 'A Critique of W. N. Pickering's *The Identity of the New Testament Text*. A Review Article.' *Westminster Theological Journal* 41 (1978), pages 397-423, reprinted in Epp and Fee 1993.

———— 'On the authenticity of John 5:3b-4', *Evangelical Quarterly*, 54 (1982), pages 207-209.

Foster, Lewis, *Selecting a Translation of the Bible*, Cincinnati, OH: Standard Publishing, 1983.

Fudge, Edward W. F., *The Fire that Consumes: The Biblical Case for Conditional Immortality*, Carlisle: Paternoster Press, 1994.

Fuller, David Otis, (ed), *Which Bible?* Grand Rapids, MI: Institute for Biblical Textual Studies, 1975.

———— ed. *True or False? The Westcott-Hort Textual Theory*

Examined. Grand Rapids, MI: Grand Rapids International Publications, 1973.

_____ ed. *Counterfeit or Genuine: Mark 16? John 8?* Grand Rapids, MI: Grand Rapids International Publications, 1975.

Glassman, E. H., *The Translation Debate*, Downers Grove: IVP, 1981.

Hasel, G., (1980) *Understanding the Living Word of God*, Mountain View, CA: Pacific Press Publishing Assoc.

Hodges, Zane C., (1968) 'The Greek Testament of the King James Version.' *Bibliotheca Sacra* 125, pages 334-45.

Hunt, Geoffrey, *About the New English Bible*, Oxford/Cambridge: OUP/CUP, 1970.

Interpreter's Dictionary of the Bible, ed. G. A. Buttrick, Nashville, TN: Abingdon, 1962.

Is, Edw F., *The King James Version Defended*. Des Moines: The Christian Research Press, 1979.

Jeremias, Joachim, *The Parables of Jesus*, rev. ed. London: SCM, 1972.

Jones, J. L., *But Which Bible?* London: Bible Reading Fellowship, 1978, 1981.

Kenyon, Frederic, (1958) *Our Bible and the Ancient Manuscripts*. London: Eyre and Spottiswoode, 5th edition, 1958. Lists disputed passage in the Gospels and Acts.

Knox, Ronald, *On Englishing the Bible*, London: Burns Oates, 1949.

Kohlenberg III, John R., 'Bible paraphrases — their possibilities and perils' *Christian Research Journal*, Spring/Summer 1994 (reprinted in *Adventist Review*, April 1995).

_____ *Words about the Word: A Guide to Choosing and Using Your Bible*, Grand Rapids, MI: Zondervan.

_____ *All About Bibles*, Oxford University Press, 1994.

Kubo, Sakae and Specht, Walter, *So Many Versions. 20th Century English Versions of the Bible*, Revised edition, Grand Rapids, MI: Zondervan, 1983.

Kuen, Alfred: See *Parole Vivante*.

Lewis, Jack P., *The English Bible from KJV to NIV*, Baker Book House, 1991.

Lindsell, Harold, *The Battle for the Bible*, Grand Rapids, MI: Zondervan, 1976.

Longman III, Tremper, *Literary Approaches to Biblical Interpretation*, Leicester: IVP, 1987.

Marcussen, Jan., 20 Theses against the New International Version, and other new perversions of the Bible based on 'Roman Catholic' and 'Sinaiaticus', and upholding the King James Version as the Holy Word of God. xc, PO Box 68, Thompsonville, IL 62890.

Margot, Jean C., 'Should a translation of the Bible be ambiguous?' *Bible Translator*, 32/4 (Oct. 1981), pages 406-413.

Mascall, E. L., *Theology and the Gospel of Christ*, London: SPCK, 1977.

Metzger, Bruce M., *The Text of the New Testament. Its Transmission, Corruption and Restoration.* Oxford: Clarendon Press, 1964.

_____ *A Textual Commentary on the Greek New Testament*, London, New York: United Bible Societies, 1971. Lists disputed passages.

_____; Dentan, Robert C.; Harrelson, Walter. *The Making of the New Revised Standard Version*, Grand Rapids, MI: Eerdmans, 1991.

Mills, Edw. F., *The King James Version Defended*, Des Moines: The Christian Research Press, 1979.

Miller, Ed L., 'The New International Version on the Prologue of John', *Harvard Theological Journal* 172 (1979), pages 305-311.

Moffatt, James, *A New Translation of the Bible*, London: Hodder & Stoughton, 1935.

Morris, Leon, *Studies in the Fourth Gospel*, Exeter: Paternoster Press, 1969.

New International Dictionary of the Christian Church, ed. J. D. Douglas, Exeter: Paternoster Press, 1974.

Nida, Eugene A., *Message and Mission. The Communication of the Christian Faith*, Pasadena, CA: William Carey Library, 1960.

Nineham, Dennis, ed. *The New English Bible Reviewed*, London: Epworth, 1965.

Opfell, Olga S., *The King James Bible Translators*, Jefferson, NC: McFarland, 1992.

Parole Vivante. La Bible transcrite pour notre temps par Alfred Kuen, Editeurs de Litterature Biblique, Chaussee de Tubize 479, B-1420 Braine-l'Alleud, Belgium.

Perry, Victor, 'Problem Passages of the New Testament in Some Modern Translations', *The Expository Times*, 87 (1975-76), pages 214, 215.

Pickering, Wilbur N., *The Identity of the New Testament Text*, Nashville, TN: Thomas Nelson, 1977.

Riplinger, G. A., *New Age Bible Versions*, Chino, CA: Chick Publications, 1993.

Sheehan, B., *Which Version Now?* Haywards Heath: Carey, 1980.

Sjoelander, Pearl & Jan Rye, 'How clear is a simplified version?' *Bible Translator*, 33/2 (April 1982), pages 223-229.

Theological Wordbook of the Old Testament, ed. R. Laird Harris, Gleason L. Archer, Bruce K. Waltke, Chicago: Moody Bible Institute, 1980.

Trinitarian Bible Society, London, publications:

Anderson, G. W., *The Greek New Testament*, 1994.

____ & D. E., *A Textual Key to the New Testament: A List of Omissions and Changes*, 1993.

____: *Why 1 John 5:7, 8 is in the Bible*, 1993.

Anon, *The Authenticity of the Last Twelve Verses of the Gospel According to Mark*, nd.

____ *God was manifested in the flesh (1 Timothy 3:16)*, London: TBS, nd.

____ *The Trinitarian Bible Society: An Introduction to the Society's Principles*, 1992.

____ *The Trinitarian Bible Society, The Constitution of the TSB*, London: TSB, 1992.

Vance, L. M., *A Brief History of English Bible Translations*, Pensecola, FL: privately printed, 1993.

Verrecchia, Jean-Claude, *La Bible, mode d'emploi*, Dammarie-les Lys Cedex: Editions Vie et Sante; Villiers-le Bel, France: Societe biblique francaise, 1995.

Vine, W. E., *Expository Dictionary of New Testament Words*, London: Oliphants, 1975.

Walden, W., *Guide to Bible Translations*, Boston, MA: Livingworks, rev. 1991.

Westcott, B. F. and Hort, F. J. A., *The New Testament in the Original Greek*, 2 vols. including Introduction and Appendices. Cambridge: Macmillan, 1882.

Westcott, B. F., Preface to *The Bible in the Church*, 1884.

White, James R., 'Is your modern translation corrupt? answering the allegations of King James Version only advocates.' *Christian Research Journal* 18 (Winter 1996) pages 21-27.

____ *The King James Only Controversy, Can you trust the modern translations?* Minneapolis: MN: Bethany House, 1995. A good defence of modern translations.

Wilkinson, Benjamin G., *Our Authorized Bible Vindicated*, Washington DC: privately published, 1930.

Wilson, John, 'The Living Bible reborn', *Christianity Today* 40/11 (Oct. 1996) pages 33-35.